engage

Issue 19 of Engage is all about living God's way. There's top teaching from Jesus (in Mark), Nehemiah and John, Proverbs and the rarely-read book of 1 Chronicles. The articles also give us top tips on walking God's way — including spotting twisted Scripture and going to church.

✳ DAILY READINGS Each day's page throws you into the Bible, to get you handling, questioning and exploring God's message to you — encouraging you to act on it and talk to God more in prayer.

THIS ISSUE: Astounding words from Jesus in **Mark;** faith in action from **Nehemiah;** weird words of wisdom in **Proverbs;** God's glorious promises in **1 Chronicles;** practical advice for Christians in **2 & 3 John.**

✳ TAKE IT FURTHER If you're hungry for more at the end of an **engage** page, turn to the **Take it further** section to dig deeper.

✳ ESSENTIAL Articles on the basics we really need to know about God, the Bible and Christianity. This issue, we get the lowdown on **eternal life for believers.**

✳ REAL LIVES True stories, revealing God at work in people's lives. This time we meet a ground-breaking **scientist** who's a Christian.

✳ TRICKY tackles those mind-bendingly tricky questions that confuse us all, as well as questions our friends bombard us with. This time we ask: **How can God forgive really evil people?**

✳ TOOLBOX is full of tools to help you understand the Bible. This issue we discover how to spot **twisted Scripture.**

✳ STUFF Articles on stuff relevant to the lives of young Christians. This issue we ask: **Why go to church?**

All of us who work on engage are passionate to see the Bible at work in people's lives. Do you want God's word to have an impact on your life? Then open your Bible, and start on the first engage study right now...

HOW TO USE engage

1 Set a time you can read the Bible every day

2 Find a place where you can be quiet and think

3 Grab your Bible, pen and a notebook

4 Ask God to help you understand what you read

5 Read the day's verses with engage, taking time to think about it

6 Pray about what you've read

BIBLE STUFF We use the NIV Bible version, so you might find it's the best one to use with engage. If the notes say **"Read Mark 9 v 2–8"**, look up Mark in the contents page at the front of your Bible. It'll tell you which page Mark starts on. Find chapter 9 of Mark, and then verse 2 of chapter 9 (the verse numbers are the tiny ones). Then start reading. Simple.

In this issue...

TEAM ENGAGE:

Words: Martin Cole   Cassie Martin   Helen Thorne
Design: Steve Devane   Andre Parker
Typo-spotting: Anne Woodcock   Nicole Carter
Edits and nervous breakdowns: Martin Cole (martin@thegoodbook.co.uk)

Jesus: A marked man

Quick! The starter's gun is about to go. Take your training gear off. Shake a leg. Flex a muscle. Do something. Just get...

ON YOUR MARKS...

You're poised for Mark's Gospel, chapters 9–11. It's vital stuff so you need to be ready. If you haven't read chapters 1–8 yet, maybe you should do that now. You'll see that Mark set out to show who Jesus is (Mark 1 v 1) and what He came to do:

"He then began to teach them that the Son of Man must suffer many things and be rejected by the elders, chief priests and teachers of the law, and that he must be killed and after three days rise again" (Mark 8 v 31).

GET SET...

So what's coming up in Mark's amazing story of Jesus' life and death? Well, in chapters 9 and 10, Jesus is on the move — teaching and healing and talking about His imminent death. His disciples still don't grasp it and Jesus presses on, knowing what's ahead.

In chapters 11 and 12, Jesus finally enters Jerusalem. But the new regime He announces isn't popular. He confronts the teachers, outsmarts the religious leaders and disappoints the crowd, who want a military hero. But things can't remain as they are because the new King's here, and His death will be a turning point for all, like it or not.

GO!

Now you've started, keep going. Pray that Jesus' astounding teaching will change you. And that the story of His incredible life will inspire you to live for Him and tell His story to others.

1 | Whiter than white

First up, it's the transfiguration. Mark shows it's about transformation + explanation = confirmation. The change in Jesus' appearance combined with His teaching confirms what He's been teaching about why He came.

Read Mark 9 v 2–8

ENGAGE YOUR BRAIN
- What amazing thing did these three disciples witness? (v2–3)

- Who else was there? (v4)

- What did God the Father say about Jesus? (v7)

- What must Jesus' followers do?

Jesus was "transfigured"; His whole appearance changed — dazzlingly pure, glorious, unique. And two Jewish heroes were there. Moses had given God's law to the Israelites and Elijah was God's messenger to His people. They had both pointed forward to someone even more important than them — Jesus.

And the disciples heard God's voice, confirming that Jesus really was His Son. So they should listen to Him. And so should we.

Read verses 9–13
- What didn't these guys understand? (v10)

- What else puzzled them? (v11)

The Jews believed that Elijah would return before the arrival of God Himself. Jesus says that John the Baptist was the "Elijah" who prepared the way for Jesus. Most people didn't realise John's importance, just as they rejected Jesus and would kill Him (v12). But here was the confirmation: the transfiguration showed who Jesus is and what He'd come for.

GET ON WITH IT
- Why do you need to listen to Jesus more?
- How do you ignore Jesus?
- What will you do about it?

PRAY ABOUT IT
Talk to God about your answers.

→ TAKE IT FURTHER
For a little more, turn to page 108.

2 | Faith the truth

Down the mountain, things weren't pretty. The rest of the disciples were arguing with the religious leaders. When Jesus arrives, it's a bit like that classroom moment when a teacher walks in to find a massive food fight...

◉ Read Mark 9 v 14–24

ENGAGE YOUR BRAIN

▶ What was the problem? (v17–18)

▶ What upset Jesus? (v19)

▶ As well as the disciples, who else had a lack of faith? (v21–23)

▶ How did he eventually show faith in Jesus? (v24)

◉ Read verses 25–32

▶ What happened? (v25–27)

▶ What mistake had the disciples made? (v28–29)

▶ Why did Jesus go into hiding? (v30–31)

▶ Why did Jesus tell them about what He was facing? (v31–32)

The disciples seemed to take for granted the power given them by Jesus. They didn't even pray about the situation — they just assumed they could deal with it themselves, without God's help. The father didn't have much faith (v24), but he *did* place his trust in Jesus. It was only then that they boy was healed.

The point is not how much faith we have (phew) but on what or who it's placed. Prayer is asking God to do for us what we can't do ourselves.

THINK IT OVER

▶ What's the first thing you do when you're hit by a crisis?

▶ What does this tell you about where you place your faith?

PRAY ABOUT IT

Ask God to help you to trust Him, always turning to Him in prayer in tough times. Thank God that you can trust Him completely.

→ TAKE IT FURTHER

Face the truth on page 108.

3 First things last

Jesus now starts spelling out to His disciples what following Him actually involves. Listen up, because He's speaking to you too.

Read Mark 9 v 33–35

ENGAGE YOUR BRAIN

- What had been the focus of the disciples' conversation?

- How do we know that Jesus already knew this?

- What does Jesus say is true greatness?

THINK IT OVER

- In what ways do you compare yourself to other people?

- Why is this not good to do?

- How exactly will you apply v35 to your life? Write in the box.

Read verses 36–37

- What does the way we treat others show?

Back then, kids were considered unimportant with no rights. Jesus was saying: *"If you want to follow me, you've got to stop putting yourself first. Serve me by serving each other and looking after people who are looked down upon and treated badly — like kids. That's how you live for me. That's true greatness."*

GET ON WITH IT

- Who do you need to be more "welcoming" towards?

- So what exactly will you do?

PRAY ABOUT IT

Talk to God very honestly about what He's taught you today.

→ TAKE IT FURTHER

More child's play on page 108.

4 | Team mates

Ever try to prove you're better or "more Christian"
that some of your friends? Ever look down on Christians
from different backgrounds and churches from yours?
If so, Jesus is about to put you in your place…

👁 **Read Mark 9 v 38–40**

ENGAGE YOUR BRAIN

▶ *What was John's problem?*

▶ *Why wasn't it a problem for Jesus?*

You've probably noticed that Christians come in all shapes and sizes , and, let's face it, some of them seem pretty weird. We won't always agree on every issue, but the bottom line is this: if someone trusts in Jesus' death to rescue them, they're your Christian brother or sister. You're in the same family.

👁 **Read verse 41**

▶ *What great promise does Jesus make?*

▶ *So how should we treat other believers?*

Jesus is very clear. Don't look down on Christians who are different from you. Don't be nice only to people similar to yourself. Anyone who trusts in Jesus to rescue them is a Christian — and you should go out of your way to be loving towards them.

GET ON WITH IT

▶ *Which Christians do you tend to avoid?*

▶ *What is Jesus' message to you?*

▶ *How can you show kindness and friendship to them?*

PRAY ABOUT IT

Think of three Christians you know who are really different from you. Thank God that He loves them and has rescued them. Pray for them that God will help them to serve Him with their lives. Pray that you can show true friendship to them.

→ TAKE IT FURTHER

Join the team on page 109.

5 | Cut it out

Sin is when we do what we want instead of
what God wants. Jesus says sin is deadly serious.

Read Mark 9 v 42

Straight-talking from Jesus. All
Christians are precious to Him and
He loves it when people get to know
Him. So anyone who causes them to
sin is in serious trouble.

Read verses 43–49

ENGAGE YOUR BRAIN

▷ What drastic action does Jesus
suggest? (v43)

▷ Why? (v43)

▷ What do you think v49 means?

Jesus isn't saying we should actually
chop off body bits if we sin! He's
pointing out how deadly serious sin
is. People who refuse to turn away
from living for themselves will be
thrown into hell. Tragic, but true.

"Everyone will be salted by fire" (v49)
probably means all Christians can
expect to be persecuted for following
Jesus. We'll all be tested in life — at

times it will feel like walking through
fire. But God uses such times to purify
us and to make us more like Jesus.

Read verse 50

Christians should be salty! They
should be tasty — standing out
from the crowd, not just living
like everyone else. Jesus should
shine through their lives. And they
shouldn't fight with each other!

GET ON WITH IT

▷ What stuff do you need to cut
out of your life?

▷ How will you do that?

▷ How can you be more salty?

PRAY ABOUT IT

Talk to God about this stuff.

THE BOTTOM LINE

If it causes you to sin, cut it out!

→ TAKE IT FURTHER

More cutting remarks on page 109.

6 | The D-word

Jesus was in the area where Herod Antipas ruled. John the Baptist had been arrested for speaking against Herod's divorce and remarriage. The Pharisees saw this as an opportunity to get Jesus into trouble.

Read Mark 10 v 1–12

ENGAGE YOUR BRAIN

▷ How was the Pharisees' question a trap? (v2)

▷ What was the Old Testament law on divorce? (v4)

▷ Why is it a long way short of what's best?

▷ What was God's intention when He created marriage? (v6–8)

▷ So what does that mean for marriage? (v9)

▷ How do verses 11–12 show marriage is for life?

Moses allowed couples to get divorced only because so many people were sinning in their marriages. It was a last resort if the situation was terrible. But many people were using Moses' law as an excuse for an easy divorce.

So, is divorce an option or not? Well, Jesus doesn't overturn Moses' permission for divorce. But the Bible is clear that divorce is only a last resort. Anyone who enters marriage thinking there is an "opt out" clause is badly mistaken.

Marriage should be for life. That is God's plan. Sadly, it doesn't always work out that way. People do get divorced and families are split up. Going against God's plan causes so much hurt.

PRAY ABOUT IT

Pray for people you know who are suffering because of divorce or family break-up. Ask God to be at the centre of their lives. And pray for married couples you know — that they'll keep going and honour God in their relationship.

→ TAKE IT FURTHER

A tiny bit more is on page 109.

9

7 | Childish behaviour

Ever felt unwanted or unimportant? Or maybe looked down on? Well, that's how kids were treated back in Jesus' time. But Jesus was about to turn this thinking upside down.

👁 Read Mark 10 v 13–16

ENGAGE YOUR BRAIN

▶ *What was the disciples' problem? (v13)*

▶ *What should they have remembered? (Mark 9 v 35–37)*

▶ *Why was Jesus so annoyed?*

▶ *What was surprsing about Jesus' words? (v15)*

▶ *How did He back up His teaching? (v16)*

Kids are important to Jesus. We shouldn't just treat them as a nuisance. We should spend time with them, and talk to them about Jesus.

GET ON WITH IT

▶ *How can you follow Jesus' example?*

▶ *Got a younger relative you can spend more time with and be more loving towards?*

▶ *Could you volunteer to help out a children's group at church?*

The "kingdom of God" (v15) means having your life ruled by God. And one day going to live with Him for ever. We can only be part of God's kingdom if we depend on Him just as little kids depend on their parents. Trusting Him for everything and letting Him have control of our lives.

PRAY ABOUT IT

Read each verse, one at a time, talking to God about it. Ask Him to help you make changes to your attitude and behaviour in response to what He's taught you today.

→ TAKE IT FURTHER

More controversy on page 109.

Money talks

We live in a time when people are obsessed with money and wealth. But it was just the same when Jesus was around. That's why money was one of the subjects He spoke about most. Listen up for some priceless teaching.

👁 Read Mark 10 v 17–22

ENGAGE YOUR BRAIN

▶ How does this guy make a good first impression? (v17–20)

▶ What was Jesus' loving but hard-hitting response? (v21)

▶ Why did Jesus ask him to give up his wealth?

We can't earn eternal life. Not with money or by living a "good life". There's no eternal inheritance for those who put money or anything else ahead of Jesus.

👁 Read verses 23–27

▶ What shocked the disciples?

▶ What amazing truth about God did Jesus tell them? (v27)

Many people think that money is the answer to their problems. But Jesus says having stacks of cash counts for nothing. In fact, money can become the focus of our lives and stop us getting to know God. But... anything is possible for God. And He can save ANYONE, whoever they are and whatever they've done.

👁 Read verses 28–31

▶ What does following Jesus involve and what's the reward? (v29–30)

Being a Christian can be costly. Sometimes we'll lose friends or our families will turn against us. We also have to turn away from things that used to be more important to us than Jesus. But in eternity, things will be very different (v31). Christians who were poor or persecuted on earth will be rewarded in eternal life!

PRAY ABOUT IT

What's the main thing God has taught you or challenged you with today? Thank Him and talk to Him about it.

→ TAKE IT FURTHER

The good life — page 109.

9 | Fame and fortune

Do you want to be famous? Do you want to be looked up to? James and John did, which led to some, um, interesting reactions. But first, another news flash from Jesus.

Read Mark 10 v 32–34

ENGAGE YOUR BRAIN

▣ Where was Jesus heading to? (v32–34)

▣ What would happen to Him?

▣ How accurate did Jesus' prediction prove to be?

Read verses 35–40

▣ What did James and John want? (v37)

"Can you drink the cup I drink?" means "Are you prepared to serve, suffer and be rejected as I will?" James and John said they were. And that's what happened — both suffered loads as they spread the gospel. But only God the Father will decide who will have positions of honour in Jesus' kingdom.

Read verses 41–45

▣ How did the other disciples react to James and John? (v41)

▣ How did Gentile rulers act? (v42)

▣ How should believers be different? (v43–44)

▣ Why did Jesus come into the world? (v45)

Greatness in the world's eyes is based on status, wealth and popularity. But greatness in God's kingdom is based on serving God and serving others. It's not about having power and bossing people around. It's about enduring hard times and injustice without complaining or turning away from God. True leaders should get their hands dirty with everyone else.

GET ON WITH IT

▣ How do you chase after status?

▣ How exactly will you be more of a servant this week?

→ TAKE IT FURTHER

Find freedom on page 109.

10 | Blind faith

Jesus has told His disciples He's on His way towards His death. He's told them that following Him means serving others and will involve suffering. Next, Jesus meets someone surprising who wants to follow Him.

👁 **Read Mark 10 v 46–52**

ENGAGE YOUR BRAIN

▶ Who did Jesus and His disciples meet?

▶ What did he call Jesus? (v47)

David had been king of God's people. God promised that one of David's descendants would be God's promised, eternal King, His Christ. This blind guy can see who Jesus is!

▶ How did people react to his shouts? (v48)

▶ What about Jesus? (v49)

▶ What did he want? (v51)

▶ Why did Jesus heal him? (v52)

▶ How did Bartimaeus respond?

Remember, Jesus is on His way to rejection and death. Following Him won't be easy — but Bartimaeus happily follows Jesus, the Son of David, who has healed him and saved him.

GET ON WITH IT

▶ Do you need for the first time to ask Jesus to heal you, to give you eternal life?

▶ Do you need to get on with following Jesus and living His way even when that brings difficulty and rejection?

PRAY ABOUT IT

Turn your answers into a prayer.

THE BOTTOM LINE

Bartimaeus shows us what Christianity's about: recognising Jesus, being saved through faith, and following Him even though it's hard.

→ TAKE IT FURTHER

No *Take it further* today.

Eternal life

Have you ever wondered what the next life is going to be like? What happens once we're dead? Do we get a harp to play? Turn into angels? Will it be fun living with Jesus? Or will it be like one giant yawn that stretches on for ever?

PERFECT PROMISE

The Bible is very clear. There will be a day when Jesus returns. No one knows when. But it's going to be amazing! When He comes back, the world as we know it will stop (2 Peter 3 v 10); people who have died in the past will be raised back to life (Revelation 20 v 11–15) and a great judgment will take place (2 Corinthians 5 v 10).

Christians don't have anything to fear because we have been forgiven for our rebellion against God (Romans 8 v 1) and our names are written in Jesus' special book of life (Revelation 21 v 27). When a believer dies they are with Jesus in paradise (Luke 23 v 43) awaiting the final day of judgment. Remember, for a Christian, dying is the start of something far better than this life (Philippians 1 v 21–23).

But what about after Jesus returns? What will we be like? And where will we be?

PERFECT HOME

Sorry if this comes as a huge disappointment, but Jesus' friends won't be sitting on a cloud for the whole of eternity. We, along with all of Jesus' other followers across the years, will be living on the new earth (2 Peter 3 v 13) in a place prepared for us by Jesus (John 14 v 1–3). When sin entered the world, God cursed the earth (Genesis 3 v 17–18). That curse will be taken away and the whole planet will be renewed and made perfect again. No more natural disasters. No wars to mess everything up. And in that world, our life is pictured as living in a brilliant city, the new Jerusalem, which has Jesus at the very centre (Revelation 21 v 1–5).

PERFECT BODY

But it's not just our environment that's going to be different, we're going to be different too! We're going to get a new body. A glorious body! (Philippians 3 v 21). After Jesus had died and risen again, Jesus' friends were able to recognise Him and touch Him (John 20 v 27) and He was able to eat too (Luke 24 v 42–43). So our new bodies won't be completely different from the ones we have now — we'll still be us! But they'll be better. They will last for ever and we won't get ill or injured (1 Corinthians 15 v 42–44).

PERFECT LIFE

And we won't be bored! There's plenty to do for the rest of eternity. We'll be working in roles that bring complete fulfilment (Revelation 7 v 15). We'll have a great time praising God (Revelation 7 v 9–10). And eternal life is described as an amazing feast of delights that will bring us pleasure beyond our wildest dreams (Luke 14 v 15–24).

PERFECT RELATIONSHIPS

Sound good? Sounds awesome! But the reason it's that brilliant is because our relationship with God will be perfect. And we will be perfect too. By far the most exciting thing about the future is that we will get to see God face to face (1 John 3 v 2). Our relationship with Him, which can be great in this life, will be complete in the next. And because there is no sin in the new world, there's no danger that we will mess it all up!

If life is tough now, why not fix your eyes on the greatness to come and remind yourself how wonderful it will be for Jesus' friends in the future?

Nehemiah

Big build-up

Remember how God's people kept on getting it wrong? Turning away from Him. Marrying the foreign women around them and worshipping their fake gods. Forgetting how God had rescued them to be His special people.

AWAY FROM HOME

Just as He'd warned them, their rebellion could only end one way, and God always keeps His promises. So He handed His people over to their enemies and they were taken off into exile in Babylon (modern-day Iraq). But that wasn't the end of the story — remember that God always keeps His promises — there would be a way back.

RETURN JOURNEY

Sure enough, after 70 years, King Darius lets some of the Jews return and that's where two guys named Ezra and Nehemiah come in. The events in the book of Nehemiah are closely linked to those in the book of Ezra — they take place straight afterwards.

BUILDING WORK

As we saw in issue 18, Ezra is concerned with re-building the temple, while Nehemiah has a God-given mission to rebuild the city of Jerusalem. But the big question is: as the city is rebuilt will the people be reformed?

Will it be a fresh start or the same old story? Will the people return to God or their old ways? Is there any hope? And what about us? Can we change? Or will we keep falling back into those same old sins time after time? Read Nehemiah and see what God has got planned!

11 | City in ruins

The good news: since King Darius had let some of the Jewish people return to Jerusalem, there had been progress. The temple was being rebuilt and things were looking positive. The bad news? Read on.

👁 **Read Nehemiah 1 v 1–4**

ENGAGE YOUR BRAIN

▷ Where is Nehemiah (v1) and what is his job? (v11)

▷ What news does Nehemiah receive? (v2–3)

▷ What is Nehemiah's reaction?

▷ Why do you think he's so bothered?

After the misery of exile, it looked as though God had forgiven His people and things were looking up. But then it started to fall apart. That's why the reality of the situation in Jerusalem hit Nehemiah so hard. But his first thought was to talk to God about it. Look at what he prays.

👁 **Read verses 5–11**

▷ What does Nehemiah know about who God is? (v5)

▷ What does he admit about himself and the rest of his people? (v6–7)

▷ What else does he remember about God? (v8–9)

▷ So what does Nehemiah ask? (v10–11)

PRAY ABOUT IT

Do you sometimes find prayer difficult? Try following Nehemiah's example. Thank God for who He is. Say sorry for the ways in which you have sinned. Ask Him to act based on His character and promises.

THE BOTTOM LINE

God always keeps His promises.

→ TAKE IT FURTHER

More info about Nehemiah can be found on page 110.

17

12 | Nervous questions

Nehemiah was devastated when he heard that God's city, Jerusalem, was lying in ruins. So he pleaded for God's help as he nervously went to ask King Artaxerxes a big favour.

Read Nehemiah 2 v 1–4

ENGAGE YOUR BRAIN

▶ Why do you think Nehemiah was so scared in v2?

Appearing before the king with a gloomy face was a total no-no. The king's servants were expected to be professionally cheerful.

▶ Amazingly what does the king ask? (v4)

▶ What is Nehemiah's first response? (v4)

Nehemiah's quick silent appeal for God's help is often called an "arrow prayer" — a quick shot upwards asking for help. Do you ever do this? When you're facing a difficult decision, awkward conversation, or are asked a tricky question about your faith?

PRAY ABOUT IT

Get into the habit of asking for God's help and power in every part of your life. 1 Peter 5 v 7 reminds us to "cast all your anxiety on him because he cares for you".

Read verses 5–10

▶ What is Nehemiah's reply to the king? (v5)

▶ Even more amazingly, how does the king react? (v6–9)

▶ Who is really behind all this?

▶ How do the enemies of the Jewish people respond to these developments? (v10)

God answered Nehemiah's prayer brilliantly! But verse 10 hints that Nehemiah might have some enemies when he starts rebuilding Jerusalem. More about that tomorrow...

→ TAKE IT FURTHER
More questions on page 110.

13 | Hope in ruins

So Nehemiah sets off on his mission to inspect the damage in Jerusalem. And yes, things are as bad as he'd feared. But he also knows that God is able to do more than we can possibly ask or imagine.

👁 Read Nehemiah 2 v 11–20

ENGAGE YOUR BRAIN

▷ How does Nehemiah begin his task? (v11–16)

▷ What does he find?

▷ Why do you think he's so secretive?

▷ What words does he use in v17 to describe the current situation?

▷ How does he describe God? (v18)

▷ How do the people of Jerusalem respond? (v18)

God prepared the way with the king and now He's clearly behind the people's enthusiasm to start rebuilding. Things are looking up.

▷ What about Sanballat and his cronies? (v19)

▷ What is Nehemiah's comeback to their taunts? (v20)

GET ON WITH IT

How do you respond when people mock you for being a Christian? Are you as confident in God's grace as Nehemiah was? Can you carry on despite opposition? It's only God's grace and power that will enable us to do so.

PRAY ABOUT IT

Get a bigger picture of God. **Read Ephesians 3 v 20–21** and let it shape your prayers today!

THE BOTTOM LINE

God's in control and always wins.

→ TAKE IT FURTHER

A new hope: page 110.

14 Gate expectations

OK, so it's time to start building, and everyone pitches in!

Skim Nehemiah 3 v 1–32

ENGAGE YOUR BRAIN

▷ Where did the building work start (see v1, v3, v6 etc)?

▷ Why were gates so important to a city?

As we'll see in the next few chapters, Jerusalem was still surrounded by enemies. Even with King Artaxerxes' backing, the city needed to be defended.

▷ How did the people group themselves to start the building work?
v3:
v7:
v8:
v28:

▷ What surprising types of people got involved? (v12)

▷ Any slackers? (v5)

GET ON WITH IT

Do you ever think you're too important to do certain tasks? Need to rethink? Remind yourself of Jesus' words in **Mark 10 v 42–45**.

▷ So how exactly will you serve God in a new way?

PRAY ABOUT IT

Christians are heading to another city — a heavenly Jerusalem, which has strong walls and beautiful gates, but these gates are never shut! Read **Revelation 21 v 10–27** and thank God that one day all threats, enemies and war will be over and we will live in perfect peace, face to face with our King.

THE BOTTOM LINE

God's people will one day live in perfect security with Him.

→ TAKE IT FURTHER

Work together on page 110.

15 Prayer in action

After such a great start, trouble is not far behind.
Yep, it's Sanballat and co. again.

👁 Read Nehemiah 4 v 1–9

ENGAGE YOUR BRAIN

▣ How did Sanballat and Tobiah try to discourage God's people?

▣ How did Nehemiah react?

▣ What exactly did he pray?

▣ Why do you think he prayed this?

Look at what Sanballat and Tobiah are mocking in v2 — not just the city but the sacrificial system and the whole worship of God. It's a very dangerous business to mock the living God.

▣ How did the building work progress despite the mockery? (v6)

▣ Had Sanballat's attempts to dishearten them worked? (v6)

▣ What tactics do Sanballat and co. resort to next? (v8)

▣ And Nehemiah and the Jews' response?

Pray and act. Prayer doesn't mean we sit back and wait. When people hassle us, we shouldn't let it get in the way of serving God. We've got to carry on living God's way.

THINK IT OVER

How do you react when people mock you or your faith? Do you lose your temper? Do you feel sorry for yourself? The great news is that we can talk to God about our problems and hand them over to Him to deal with them.

PRAY ABOUT IT

What do you need to ask God to enable you to do today? Ask Him and then get on with it!

THE BOTTOM LINE

God's people will face opposition.

→ TAKE IT FURTHER

Take action and go to page 110.

16 | Prepared for battle

God's people are rebuilding Jerusalem and are about to face more opposition. Will the people start to crack just like the walls (groan)? Not on Nehemiah's watch!

👁 Read Nehemiah 4 v 10–15

ENGAGE YOUR BRAIN

▶ What problems are the people facing? (v10–13)

▶ What is Nehemiah's two-pronged response? (v13–14)

▶ Why will remembering who God is help them?

▶ Who wrecked their enemies' plans? (v15)

👁 Read verses 16–23

▶ What system does Nehemiah put in place to ensure the building work continues and is protected? (v16–20)

▶ What was he confident of? (v20)

Under huge pressure, the work went on. Starting something is all very well, but keeping going through the tough times until it is finished is what counts. The great news is that whenever life seems too hard to keep going as a Christian, we have God with us on our side, fighting for us!

PRAY ABOUT IT

The Bible says God's people should always be ready for battle — prepared to fight against the devil's schemes and temptations. Read **Ephesians 6 v 10–18** and pray through the armour you need to put on today, remembering that prayer itself is part of our weaponry.

THE BOTTOM LINE

Our God will fight for us.

→ TAKE IT FURTHER

Fight on to page 110.

17 | Trouble within

We've seen Nehemiah and his team of builders facing heavy opposition from enemies outside the city. But there were big problems inside the city too.

Read Nehemiah 5 v 1–5

ENGAGE YOUR BRAIN

▶ What was the problem? (v1–4)

▶ What had they resorted to? (v5)

Shockingly, it was the Jewish officials, placed in charge by Artaxerxes' regime, who were extracting huge amounts of money from their own people in tax.

Read verses 6–13

Usury is lending money at extortionate interest rates.

▶ What does Nehemiah accuse the VIPs of? (v7–8)

▶ What does he want them to do? (v9–11)

▶ What happens? (v12–13)

Nehemiah said God's people shouldn't cheat each other in this way. Instead, gifts and generosity towards the needy was the way forward.

Read verses 14–19

▶ How does Nehemiah set an example of how God wants His people to be? (v14–18)

▶ Was Nehemiah entitled to money and great food?

▶ Why didn't he enforce his rights?

PRAY ABOUT IT

The whole earth belongs to the Lord and yet He generously gives us life, food, friends, family and salvation. Thank God for His generosity, especially in sending Jesus who *"though he was rich, yet for your sakes he became poor, so that you through his poverty might become rich"* (2 Corinthians 8 v 9).

THE BOTTOM LINE

God is generous. So we should be generous too.

→ TAKE IT FURTHER

More on page 111.

18 | Fighting talk

The work on the wall is going well though not finished yet. But Sanballat, Tobiah and co. are still trying to derail the work and intimidate Nehemiah and God's people.

Read Nehemiah 6 v 1–7

ENGAGE YOUR BRAIN

▶ Where has the work got to? (v1)

▶ What are Sanballat and his cronies up to? (v2)

▶ What is Nehemiah's reply? (v3–4)

▶ How persistent are they?

▶ How do they become sneakier in v5–7?

▶ Why might this approach work for them?

Not only is Nehemiah accused (falsely) of treason but it's in an open letter that anyone can read. Sanballat is trying to intimidate and undermine all those working with Nehemiah.

Read verses 8–14

▶ How does Nehemiah respond? (v8)

▶ Who does he turn to? (v9)

▶ What tactic do God's enemies try next? (v10–14)

▶ Does Nehemiah see through them? (v11–13)

GET ON WITH IT

The apostle Peter gives this advice to Christians facing false accusations: *"Live such good lives among the pagans that, though they accuse you of doing wrong, they may see your good deeds and glorify God on the day he visits us"* (1 Peter 2 v 12).

Ask for God's help to do that in your situation today.

→ TAKE IT FURTHER

Intimidation and anxiety on page 111.

24

19 | Finished!

Have you ever seen a building site in action?
Houses or offices can go up fairly quickly,
but they've got nothing on Nehemiah's gang.

👁 **Read Nehemiah 6 v 16–19**

ENGAGE YOUR BRAIN

▷ How long had the whole project taken? (v15)

▷ What did that show about the whole thing? (v16)

▷ How did it affect the surrounding enemy nations?

Seven weeks is a seriously impressive timescale for this amount of work. No long tea breaks for Nehemiah's team. They have been motivated and dedicated despite major opposition. Clearly God is the one at work. But it's not all plain sailing.

▷ What new problem does Nehemiah face? (v17–19)

Tobiah is using his family ties to manipulate people within the city. A prime example of why marrying outside of God's people was such a bad idea. Keep this in mind; it's going to be a major issue later on in Nehemiah.

👁 **Read Nehemiah 7 v 1–3**

▷ Once the work is complete are the troubles at an end? (7 v 1–3)

▷ What are the criteria Nehemiah uses to decide who should be in charge of defending the city? (v2)

PRAY ABOUT IT

Hanani and Hananiah feared the Lord. Proverbs 9 v 10 tells us that: *"The fear of the Lord is the beginning of wisdom"*. Ask God to help you to fear, love and respect Him and value His opinion above anyone else's.

THE BOTTOM LINE

Fear the Lord.

→ TAKE IT FURTHER

Grab some more on page 111.

20 | Listed building

The city walls are rebuilt, but Jerusalem is still a bit on the empty side. Time for operation repopulation!

Skim Nehemiah 7 v 4–73

ENGAGE YOUR BRAIN

▷ What is the situation in v4?
▷ What does God move Nehemiah to do about it? (v5)
▷ Why do you think he starts with those who were first to return?
▷ What does that show about their hearts as far as God's promises and God's city go?
▷ How does Nehemiah list them? What groupings does he use?
▷ What does that show about his concerns (eg: v43, v46)?
▷ Why do you think he is particularly concerned about the priests being pure? (v63–65)

One of the big problems before the exile was corrupt worship. So Nehemiah is taking no chances with priests from a shady background. They're out until they've been properly approved. Urim and Thumin (v65) was a kind of lot-drawing only done by the priests.

▷ How do the people contribute towards the building programme? (v70–72)
▷ Where do the people settle? (v73)

Jerusalem hasn't been repopulated yet, but a clear record has been established of which of God's people could be part of it. Incidentally, it's the same list as in Ezra chapter 2.

PRAY ABOUT IT

In Revelation 21 v 3 we read about the New Jerusalem where *"the dwelling of God is with men, and he will live with them. They will be his people, and God himself will be with them and be their God"*. Thank God for that wonderful promise made possible because of what Jesus has done for us.

THE BOTTOM LINE

All of God's people get to live in the New Jerusalem!

→ TAKE IT FURTHER

Want more? Go to page 111.

Proverbs: Living for God

We're going to spend a few days in Proverbs. Unlike most Bible books, there's no story flowing through it and one verse may be very different from the next. But there is so much God wants to say to you through this unique book.

◉ **Read Proverbs 17 v 1–10**

ENGAGE YOUR BRAIN

▣ What are we told about words?
  v4:
  v7:
  v9:

▣ What do you think v3 is saying?

Proverbs is full of advice about what comes out of our mouths. Words are so important; we must be careful what we listen to and how we use language. Lies and evil words have no place in a Christian's life. Don't listen to them and stop uttering them. And if someone messes up and sins, don't gossip about it. Showing love to others means moving on, not holding grudges or telling everyone about it.

Verse 3 talks about fire being used to refine precious metals. It doesn't destroy them. In the same way, the Lord uses tough and testing experiences to improve us and help us to become more like Jesus.

◉ **Skim read verses 11–28**

▣ Which of these proverbs leap out at you?

▣ Which one should you act on?

▣ Any you really don't understand?

▣ Who could you ask to explain it?

▣ Will you?

▣ And what else are we told about words in v14 and 27–28?

PRAY ABOUT IT

Talk to God about anything He's challenged you about today. And ask Him to refine you, especially in the way you use words.

→ **TAKE IT FURTHER**

Follow the fool to page 112.

22 Hearing aid

There's loads about ears and mouths in this chapter of Proverbs. So listen carefully and look out for any proverbs about listening and speaking.

Read Proverbs chapter 18

ENGAGE YOUR BRAIN

▷ What's the mark of a fool's speech and listening? (v2, 13)
▷ Why is that a problem? (v6–7)
▷ How is gossip described in v8?
▷ How should we be different? (v15)

It's an easy trap to fall into. We can be so keen to get our opinion across that we don't listen to others (v13). If we want to learn, we'll take time to listen and not talk so much (v2).

So here's our test to see how closed your ears are. Be honest and score one point for each "Yes".

• Do you ever answer without listening?
• Do you enjoy telling others what you think?
• Do you find it hard to just listen to someone else without taking over the conversation?

• In Christian meetings, does your mind wander or do you listen to what you're being taught?
• Do you often interrupt?

Scores

7: Cheat!
5–6: Oh dear. Start listening up!
2–4: Not bad, but work at "open ears, closed mouth".
0–1: You should be writing this study.

GET ON WITH IT

▷ Who should you listen more to?
▷ How can you work on not taking over conversations?

PRAY ABOUT IT

Pray about any issues that have come up today.

THE BOTTOM LINE

Open your ears, close your mouth.

→ TAKE IT FURTHER

Listen up on page 112.

23 | Wise words from God

God has something to say to you today. It might be about friendship, lies, obedience, living for God, or something completely different. Right now, ask God to speak clearly to you through this chapter of Proverbs.

👁 Read Proverbs 19 v 1–15

ENGAGE YOUR BRAIN
▷ What kinds of people have loads of friends? (v4, 6–7)
▷ Why?
▷ What's the warning for liars? (v5)

GET ON WITH IT
▷ How do you choose your friends?
▷ Which outsiders will you make an effort to befriend?
▷ When do you tend to lie?
▷ How can you be more honest?
▷ Is God saying anything to you in v10–15?
▷ If so, what do you need to do?

👁 Read verses 16–19
▷ Why should we obey wise instruction? (v16, 20)
▷ What if we don't? (v16, 27)
▷ Whose plans should we follow? (v21)
▷ What's the eventual reward for living God's way? (v23)
▷ Anything else that jumps out at you from v16–29?

What's the main thing God has taught you today?

What will you do about it?

PRAY ABOUT IT
Respond to God's teaching.
Talk honestly with Him.

→ TAKE IT FURTHER
Keep on giving – page 112.

24 | Just the one

👁 **Read Proverbs 20 v 1–5**

ENGAGE YOUR BRAIN

▶ *Which verse here seems most relevant to you?*

If a verse grabbed you, read it again, thoughtfully. If none did, don't worry about it; just read the next section.

👁 **Read verses 6–10**

▶ *Is there a verse in this section that's slapped you hard?*

Think how real your professions of love are (v6). Or whether your conscience is clear (v9).

👁 **Read verses 11–17**

If a verse has already stood out to you, don't hunt for another. If not, is there one here? For example, do you have problems getting up? (v13)

THINK IT OVER

Which verse has really hit you today? In the first box, write it in your own words. Modernise it if you need to.

Now write down what it is about the verse that really speaks to you.

PRAY ABOUT IT

Now ask God to help you understand His word and obey it.

→ TAKE IT FURTHER

More thoughts on page 112.

25 | God's searchlight

Time for one more glimpse at Proverbs before catching up with Jesus in Mark's Gospel. So get ready for God to speak to you again through these powerful proverbs.

👁 **Read Proverbs 20 v 18–22**

ENGAGE YOUR BRAIN

▶ What's the advice about chatterboxes? (v19)

▶ Why?

▶ How seriously does God take us badmouthing our parents? (v20)

▶ What is v22 saying to you?

▶ How do you get that wrong sometimes?

▶ What do you need to do?

Got the message yet? Be careful about what you say and who you listen to. And don't seek revenge. If someone wrongs you, talk to God about it and then leave justice to Him. And patiently wait for God to deal with the situation.

👁 **Read verses 23–30**

▶ Which proverb surprises you?

▶ Why?

▶ Which one is most relevant to your life right now?

▶ So what will you do about it?

👁 **Read verse 27 again**

▶ What's the big truth here?

▶ How should it affect the way you live?

GET ON WITH IT

Look back over the last 5 studies. Somewhere, note down exactly what God has been saying to you and exactly what you'll do about it. If you're feeling brave, show it to another Christian so they can check how you're getting along.

PRAY ABOUT IT

Make sure you talk to God about these things every day.

➔ **TAKE IT FURTHER**

No *Take it further* today.

Scientist and believer

The American scientist Francis Collins is leader of the Human Genome Project, a multibillion-dollar research programme aimed at understanding human nature and healing our inherited disorders. And he's a Christian. But can science and Christianity go hand-in-hand?

PART OF GOD'S PLAN

Francis says he finds no conflict between the worlds of science and Christianity: "As the director of the Human Genome Project, I have led a group of scientists to read out the 3.1 billion letters of the human genome, our own DNA instruction book. As a believer, I see DNA — the information molecule of all living things — as God's language, and the elegance and complexity of our own bodies and the rest of nature as a reflection of God's plan.

SEARCHING QUESTIONS

"I did not always think like this. As a graduate student in physical chemistry in the 1970s, I was an atheist, finding no reason to believe in the existence of any truths outside of mathematics, physics and chemistry. But then I went to medical school, and encountered life and death issues at the bedsides of my patients. Challenged by one of those patients, who asked: 'What do you believe, doctor?', I began searching for answers.

"I had to admit that the science I loved so much was powerless to answer questions such as 'What is the meaning of life?' 'Why am I here?" 'Why do humans have a moral sense?' 'What happens after we die?'

"I had always assumed that faith was based on purely emotional and irrational arguments. I was astounded to discover, initially in the writings of C.S. Lewis, that one could build a very strong case for the plausibility of the existence of God on purely rational

grounds. It became hard to defend my previous atheistic belief that "I know there is no God".

"But reason alone cannot prove the existence of God. Ultimately, a leap of faith is required. For me, that leap came in my 27th year, after a search to learn more about God's character led me to the person of Jesus Christ. Here was a person with remarkably strong historical evidence of His life, who made astounding statements about loving your neighbour. His claims about being God's Son seemed to demand a decision about whether He was deluded or the real thing. After resisting for nearly two years, I found it impossible to go on living in such a state of uncertainty, and I became a follower of Jesus.

SCIENCE VS CHRISTIANITY

"So, some have asked, doesn't your brain explode? Can you both pursue an understanding of how life works using the tools of genetics and molecular biology, and worship a creator God? Aren't evolution and faith in God incompatible? Can a scientist believe in miracles like the resurrection?

"Actually, I find no conflict here, and neither apparently do the 40 percent of working scientists who claim to be believers. I believe that evolution by descent from a common ancestor is true. [Many Christians disagree on this.] But why couldn't this be God's plan for creation?

"I have found there is a wonderful harmony in the complementary truths of science and faith. The God of the Bible is also the God of the genome. God can be found in the cathedral or in the laboratory. By investigating God's majestic and awesome creation, science can actually be a means of worship."

26 Jesus: A marked man

Jesus and His 12 disciples arrived in Jerusalem just in time for the Passover feast. A huge time of celebration. But Jesus also knew He was walking ever closer to His death.

👁 Read Mark 11 v 1–7

ENGAGE YOUR BRAIN

▷ What was Jesus' bizarre instruction? (v2–3)

▷ What happened? (v4–7)

▷ Why? (see Zechariah 9 v 9)

Old Testament prophet Zechariah said that the one riding into Jerusalem on a donkey would be God's chosen King — the Saviour of the world.

👁 Read verses 8–11

▷ What did people do as Jesus entered into the city?

▷ What did they say?

▷ What was their opinion of Jesus?

Jerusalem was packed with people ready to celebrate the Passover feast. They welcomed Jesus like royalty, praising Him. There was a huge buzz created by His entry — could this be the Messiah they'd been waiting for? Well, yes, He was! But Jesus wasn't the kind of King most people were expecting.

Hosanna means "Lord, save us". They were right that Jesus was their King, who'd come to save them. But they thought He'd save them by fighting the Romans. They didn't realise that Jesus had come to die on the cross to save them from their sins. A few days later, another crowd would be shouting for Jesus to be killed!

PRAY ABOUT IT

Spend time praising King Jesus. Thank Him that He came as King to save His people from sin and punishment in hell.

THE BOTTOM LINE

Praise King Jesus! Welcome Him!

➡ TAKE IT FURTHER

Full marks for turning to page 113.

27 Turning the tables

Why is a fig tree like a temple? Well, they're both fruity... no... ummm... maybe it's because... no... that's not it. I give up. Let's see if Jesus can shed any light on this riddle.

Read Mark 11 v12–14

ENGAGE YOUR BRAIN

▶ *What did Jesus want?*

▶ *What did He get?*

▶ *So what did He do?*

Now keep that little fig story in mind as Jesus enters the temple.

Read verses 15–19

▶ *What did Jesus do in the temple? (v15–16)*

▶ *Why? (v17)*

▶ *What two different effects did Jesus have on people? (v18)*

Clever. The story of the fig tree illustrates what would happen to the temple. The fig tree had loads of leaves but no fruit. Likewise, the temple and the people who used it were all show, but with no fruit. By cursing the fruitless fig tree, Jesus was spelling out the end for the temple.

Jesus was furious! The temple was the place where God was present among His people. But instead of worshipping God, these guys used the temple to rip people off. They were also robbing God of the worship He should get in His house.

The temple's days were numbered. Jesus would soon die and be raised back to life. After that, things would change. *Everyone* would be able to get to know God, not just Jewish people. And people wouldn't have to go to the temple to meet God any more. Jesus' death would remove the barrier between us and God, so that *anyone* can now meet Him *anywhere*.

PRAY ABOUT IT

Thank God that because of Jesus, we can now get to know Him personally.

→ TAKE IT FURTHER

More on Jesus' temple fury on page 113.

28 Figs and faith

The fruitless fig tree and the incident with the money changers have shown that the temple wasn't all it was cracked up to be. Or rather, God's people were not so hot. Now Jesus uses the fig tree to make another big point.

Read Mark 11 v 20–25

ENGAGE YOUR BRAIN

▷ Why was Peter amazed?

▷ Why shouldn't he have been suprised?

Jesus is God — if He says a fig tree will wither, of course it will. Like Peter, we should have more faith in God (v22).

▷ How much is God able and willing to answer? (v23–24)

▷ What should our expectation be when we pray? (v24)

Amazing stuff. Anything is possible in God's power. If we truly believe that God can answer our prayers, He will answer. We've got to have faith.

THINK IT OVER

▷ When you pray, do you have faith that God will answer?

▷ What makes you doubt?

▷ How will you pray differently today?

ENGAGE YOUR BRAIN

▷ What else is vital when we pray?

▷ Who are you holding a grudge against?

▷ Will you deal with it right now?

PRAY ABOUT IT

Read today's verses again and then spend an extended time in prayer, putting Jesus' teaching into practice.

THE BOTTOM LINE

You've got to have faith.

TAKE IT FURTHER

A little bit more on page 113.

29 | Trick questions

Jesus is in Jerusalem and the Jewish leaders don't like what He's been doing and saying. They especially didn't enjoy Jesus taking over in the temple and throwing out the rip-off merchants. They're after His blood.

👁 **Read Mark 11 v 27–33**

ENGAGE YOUR BRAIN

▷

▷ *Who cornered Jesus? (v27)*

▷ *What did they want to know?*

If Jesus answered: "I'm doing this with God's authority", they'd charge Him with blasphemy (which led to the death penalty). If He said: "No one has given me authority to do this", they'd show Him to be a massive fraud.

▷ *What was clever about Jesus' reply? (v29–32)*

▷ *So what happened? (v33)*

John the Baptist told people to get ready for Jesus, God's promised King. So the question is: Did John's message about Jesus come from God or not?

If they said it did come from God, they'd be admitting that Jesus was

from God too! But if they said it wasn't from God, they feared the crowds would turn on them. So they refused to answer the question. And so did Jesus.

PRAY ABOUT IT

▷ *Who do you think Jesus really is?*

If you're not sure, ask God to reveal the real Jesus to you. If you trust Him as your King, tell Him so and thank Him for what He's done for you.

➔ **TAKE IT FURTHER**
No *Take it further* today.

30 Horror story

The Jewish leaders are out to get Jesus. And they'll hate Him even more after listening to this powerful parable. See if you can work out what it's a picture of.

Read Mark 12 v 1–9

The vineyard was an Old Testament picture of God's people, the Israelites. The owner is God. The servants are God's prophets. The tenants are the Jewish leaders. The son is Jesus. And the whole story is a speedy history of Israel: v1–5 is the past; v6–8 is the present; v9 is the future.

ENGAGE YOUR BRAIN

▷ How had the Jews treated God's messengers in the past?

▷ How were they treating Jesus and what would they do to Him?

▷ What would happen to them in the future?

Read verses 10–12

▷ What does v10–11 tell us about Jesus?

▷ How did the leaders react to all this? (v12)

God's people, Israel, and its leaders had rejected God's prophets down the centuries. And now they'd rejected God's own Son. So God turned to people who would accept Jesus as the world's Ruler and would live lives that produced fruit for God. They would now be God's true people.

THINK IT OVER

It's easy for us to criticise these Jews for rejecting Jesus. But let's not miss the truth for us: rejecting Jesus is serious. And we reject Jesus when we think we know better than God and live our own way, not God's.

PRAY ABOUT IT

▷ In what areas of life are you in danger of doing that?

Talk it over with God right now.

TAKE IT FURTHER

More from God's prophets on page 113.

31 | Taxing question

Ever been too busy basking in someone's flattery or "kind" words to notice that they're actually stabbing you in the back? Jesus' enemies were ganging together to trap Him. Very politely.

👁 Read Mark 12 v 13–17

ENGAGE YOUR BRAIN

▶ How did they flatter Jesus?

▶ What was their trick question?

▶ What did Jesus know was going on? (v15)

▶ What's so brilliant about Jesus' answer? (v16–17)

The Pharisees were Jewish leaders who hated their Roman rulers. The Herodians supported Herod, the local Roman ruler. With this question, there was no way Jesus could please both sides. If Jesus said: "Yes, pay Caesar's taxes", the Pharisees could accuse Him of siding with the Romans against the Jews. If Jesus said "No, don't pay them", the Herodians could claim He was breaking Roman law.

Jesus' answer was perfect. It's right to pay taxes and obey the government's laws. But also there's a higher loyalty.

Humans bear the image of God — and so must give God the obedience He deserves.

GET ON WITH IT

▶ In what ways do you disobey authority?

▶ In what specific ways can you give God what belongs to Him?
time:
money:
abilities:
your life:

PRAY ABOUT IT

Talk your answers over with God, committing yourself to doing them.

THE BOTTOM LINE

Give to God what belongs to Him.

➡ **TAKE IT FURTHER**

Money matters on page 113.

32 Wife after death

The religious groups are lining up to trick Jesus. Next up are the Sadducees, a group of rich Jews who didn't believe in resurrection — eternal life for believers after death. Which makes their question extra weird.

Read Mark 12 v 18–25

ENGAGE YOUR BRAIN

▷ What two things were wrong with the Sadducees' question? (v24)

▷ What had they failed to realise about life after death? (v25)

It doesn't seem very likely, does it? One woman marrying seven brothers, one after the other? The Sadducees thought this bizarre question would beat Jesus. They even quoted Moses. Surely Jesus couldn't get out of this one. But Jesus didn't waste much time with the Sadd' guys' question.

Of course eternal life won't be the same as this life. We'll have brand new bodies. And we won't be married — we'll be living with Jesus. The Bible tells us that marriage is a picture of the close relationship between Jesus and His people.

Read verses 26–27

▷ How did Jesus answer claims that there is no life after death?

The Sadducees believed that only the first five books of the Bible (written by Moses) were true. Jesus cleverly used Moses to show they were wrong — there is life after death. Just like Abraham, Isaac and Jacob, all believers will go to live with God. We'll have brand new bodies and there won't be marriage. There will be something better! Life with Jesus.

SHARE IT

▷ As a Christian, what can you say to friends who claim there's no life after death?

▷ What can you tell them about the hope you have of eternal life?

PRAY ABOUT IT

Thank God for the great hope of a perfect future that Christians have, because of Jesus.

TAKE IT FURTHER

More about the afterlife on page 114.

33 | Great question!

Question time isn't over yet. Next in line to talk to Jesus is a teacher of the (Old Testament) law. But this one doesn't seem to be out to trap Jesus. He actually wants to learn from Him.

👁 **Read Mark 12 v 28–34**

ENGAGE YOUR BRAIN

▷ What was the question that Old Testament experts debated? (v28)

▷ How did Jesus answer? (v29–31)

▷ How would you sum that up in 8 words or less?

▷ What did the questioner recognise? (v32–33)

▷ How did Jesus encourage him? (v34)

THINK IT OVER

▷ What does it mean to love God...

with all your heart?

with all your soul?

with all your mind?

with all your strenth?

God expects us to love Him with all of our being! All our thoughts, words and actions should be for God. It sounds impossible, but it's what we should aim for and long to do. And through the Holy Spirit, God enables us to love Him more and more in every part of our lives.

GET ON WITH IT

Pick three people you know: one you love, one you dislike and one you don't know very well. For each of them, think what it would mean to love them as you love yourself. Then figure out one way you can do this. And do it!

PRAY ABOUT IT

Ask God to help you to love Him with your whole life. And ask for His help in doing the stuff you decided in the *Get on with it* section.

→ **TAKE IT FURTHER**

A tiny bit more on page 114.

Son of David

Over the last week, we've seen Jesus' enemies ganging together, asking Him ridiculous questions, trying to trap Him into slipping up. They failed miserably. So now Jesus has a difficult question for them.

Read Mark 12 v 35–37

ENGAGE YOUR BRAIN

▶ What was Jesus' tricky question? (v35)

The Jewish people were waiting for the Christ to come and rescue them. Jesus claimed to be the Christ. The Jewish Old Testament experts knew the Christ would come from King David's family. So they didn't believe he would be God too.

▶ How would you sum up Jesus' argument?

▶ If you're not sure, how could you find out what Jesus meant?

Jesus was quoting Psalm 110. By calling the Christ "my Lord", David is saying that the Christ is also God. The Jewish leaders hadn't worked this out. But we know that Jesus is the Christ, who rescues His people. And that He's God too!

Jesus had been called "Son of David", so they knew He was challenging them to accept Him as the Christ. They refused to do that, and the next time they met, it would be to arrest Him.

THINK IT OVER

People still offer every excuse and argument possible to avoid accepting Jesus as King. Do you make that mistake too? How about people around you?

PRAY ABOUT IT

Thank God that Jesus is the Christ — the perfect King who God sent to rescue us from the punishment we deserve for our sins. Ask God to use you to get the message of Jesus across to those who refuse to believe. And pray that you'll live in a way that shows Jesus is King of your life.

TAKE IT FURTHER

Psing a psalm on page 114.

35

Fake or faithful?

The religious leaders have been giving Jesus a hard time, trying to trap Him with trick questions. But now the boot is on the other foot as Jesus shows up their shallowness.

👁 Read Mark 12 v 38–40

ENGAGE YOUR BRAIN

▷ What did Jesus reveal about the teachers of the law?
▷ What would happen to them?

These men were supposed to teach people God's word. But they abused their power, seeking popularity and praise. They even cheated people out of money. God would punish them.

👁 Read verses 41–44

▷ What was special about what the widow did? (v42)
▷ Why did Jesus say she'd given more than the rich guys?

This woman had no earning power — her husband had died and women didn't do paid work back then. She was looked down on and treated as a second-class citizen. But Jesus looks at the heart. The widow gave all she had — showing her love for God and trusting in Him for the future (even her next meal). She didn't keep one coin for herself. But the teachers were just trying to look impressive.

THINK IT THROUGH

▷ What do you do to get praise or attention?
▷ Do you view your money as belonging to you or to God?
▷ How is that shown in how you use it?

GET ON WITH IT

You'll soon discover how much of a hold money has on you when you start giving it away.

▷ How will you use your money to serve God?

PRAY ABOUT IT

Talk to God right now. Be honest about stuff you've been trying to hide from Him. Talk to Him about your attitude to money and giving.

TAKE IT FURTHER

Further stuff on money on page 114.

36 | Psalms: Sing it loud

Before we catch up with Nehemiah, let's have a musical interlude. Two psalms full of praise to God. Today's psalm is a good one. Imagine the Israelites singing it to God as you read the words.

👁 Read Psalm 135 v 1–4

ENGAGE YOUR BRAIN

▶ What are God's people told to do? (v1–3)

▶ Why? (v4)

Jacob and *Israel* are both names for God's Old Testament people. He had chosen them and treasured them — they had every reason to sing God's praises. But how could they be certain He'd chosen them?

👁 Read verses 5–21

▶ What does v5–7 tell us about God?

▶ What have the Israelites seen God do? (v8–12)

▶ So what could they be sure of? (v13–14)

▶ Why is it crazy to worship anything but God? (v15–18)

▶ What should God's people be quick to do? (v19–21)

How can God's people know He's chosen them? Well, we can look at God's character. We read in the Bible of His great care for His people. We can look at what He's done for us in the past and notice how He's looking after us now. And we can hold on to His promises. Especially the promise that all who trust in Jesus are part of God's eternal family.

THINK IT OVER

▶ So... what reasons do we have for praising God?

PRAY ABOUT IT

What are you waiting for?

→ TAKE IT FURTHER

No *Take it further* today.

44

37 | Lasting love

Time for another song to God. I think you'll
get the main message of this one very quickly...

👁 Read Psalm 136 v 1–9

ENGAGE YOUR BRAIN

▶ God is full of endless love (v1).
How do we know that's true?

▶ What's one area we should thank
and praise Him for? (v4–9)

PRAY ABOUT IT

We can see God's love and care in
creation. Quick, go outside, look
around and praise God.

👁 Read verses 10–22

▶ How do we see God's love for His
people in Old Testament history?
v10–15:
v16:
v17–20:
v21–22:

👁 Read verses 23–26

▶ What has God done for us?
v23:
v24:
v25:

There's so much evidence that God
loves you! Just look at His amazing
creation. Such a beautiful world and
He's put us in charge of it. We can
open our Bibles and read how God
has cared for His people — so many
incredible examples. And we can look
back at our own lives, remembering
how God has rescued us (v24) and
how He meets our everyday needs
(v25). God loves you.

PRAY ABOUT IT

God's everlasting love to us is shown
in the fact that He's Creator, Rescuer,
Conqueror and Friend. There's only
one right response — to thank Him.
And now's a good time to start...

THE BOTTOM LINE

God's love endures for ever.

→ TAKE IT FURTHER

Let's go back to the beginning...
page 115.

How can God forgive really evil people?

Each issue in TRICKY, we tackle those mind-bendingly difficult questions that confuse us all, as well as questions that friends bombard us with to catch us off guard. This time we ask: How can God forgive really evil people? Would God really forgive a paedophile or a mass murderer?

UNDESERVED FORGIVENESS

The shocking extent of God's generosity towards sinful human beings was demonstrated for us again and again by Jesus, and perhaps never more so than when He was hanging between two criminals, suffering the most painful death imaginable.

"One of the criminals who hung there hurled insults at him: 'Aren't you the Christ? Save yourself and us!' But the other criminal rebuked him. 'Don't you fear God,' he said, 'since you are under the same sentence? We are punished justly, for we are getting what our deeds deserve. But this man has done nothing wrong.' Then he said, 'Jesus, remember me when you come into your kingdom.' Jesus answered him, 'I tell you the truth, today you will be with me in paradise'" (Luke 23 v 39–43).

A person executed on a cross was no petty criminal. This was reserved for the lowest of the low. The most disparaged and despised members of society. People that modern-day tabloids would describe as evil.

And what does it take for Jesus to forgive such a person? Nothing but an acknowledgement of guilt ("We are punished justly, for we are getting what our deeds deserve") and an expression of trust ("Jesus, remember me when you come into your kingdom").

INCREDIBLE OFFER

But how can God forgive evil so readily? Well, there is nothing cheap about the forgiveness God offers in Jesus Christ. He paid for it in suffering, bloodshed and death. This wasn't just a man dying, but one who was God (John 1 v 1). God's perfect justice demands that terrible evil is paid for with an equally terrible penalty. Christ's cross was the utmost terrible penalty, sufficient to pay for all sin, however evil. And God cannot be fooled. It's not as if God is hoodwinked if someone "pretends" to say sorry, just to get off the hook. As Psalm 44 says, God "knows the secrets of the heart".

So how can God forgive child molesters and serial killers? The bottom line is this: if you sincerely long to be forgiven, it doesn't matter what you've done, or how late in life you put your trust in Jesus. His death on the cross is more than enough to earn you that forgiveness, and ensure that you spend eternity with Him "in paradise".

AMAZING GENEROSITY

Jesus tells the story of a landowner who pays people to work in his vineyard. Some he employs early in the day, others "at the eleventh hour". Then the time comes to pay the men:

"The workers who were hired about the eleventh hour came and each received a denarius. So when those came who were hired first, they expected to receive more. But each one of them also received a denarius. When they received it, they began to grumble against the landowner.

'These men who were hired last worked only one hour,' they said, 'and you have made them equal to us who have borne the burden of the work and the heat of the day.'

"But he answered one of them, 'Friend, I am not being unfair to you. Didn't you agree to work for a denarius? Take your pay and go. I want to give the man who was hired last the same as I gave you. Don't I have the right to do what I want with my own money? Or are you envious because I am generous?' "
(Matthew 20 v 9–15)

God's generosity is such that he gives freely to whoever he chooses. We may feel that we deserve God's forgiveness far more than other people. But the fact is that none of us deserves anything from God. We should be profoundly grateful for his generosity, not find ways to begrudge it.

Taken from "If You Could Ask God One question" by Paul Williams and Barry Cooper. Available from The Good Book Company website.

47

38 Nehemiah: Big build-up

Jerusalem's walls have been rebuilt. Now on to the issue of rebuilding and reforming the lives of God's people. Will the damage be as quick and easy to repair?

Read Nehemiah 8 v 1–12

ENGAGE YOUR BRAIN

The real work begins with the reading and hearing of God's word.

▶ Who gets to listen? (v2–3)

▶ How long does it last?

▶ How would you describe the people's attitude? (v3, 5, 6)

▶ How does Ezra ensure everyone understands what is being read? (v7–8)

▶ How many times does the word "understand" appear in these verses?

Good system. Everyone hears God's word together, and then smaller groups really dig deeper, making sure they understand it. Does your church do that?

GET ON WITH IT

Are you part of a small group (CU, youth group, home group, Bible study) that really gets involved with understanding God's word and applying it to your life? If not, is there one you could join?

▶ Why do you think the people responded to the reading of the Law in the way they did? (v9)

▶ What are they encouraged to do instead? (v10–12)

▶ Why?

PRAY ABOUT IT

God's word can often make us sad as we see our sin more clearly, but it also shows us how wonderful God is. Spend some time now celebrating how great our God is.

➡ TAKE IT FURTHER

Don't worry, be happy — page 115.

39 | Branching out

There was plenty to discover in God's long-neglected Law. And one of the first things the people did was to celebrate a festival. With some DIY thrown in too.

👁 **Read Nehemiah 8 v 13–18**

ENGAGE YOUR BRAIN

▶ What did the people discover (or re-discover) in the Book of the Law? (v14–15)

The Festival of Booths was when everyone camped out for a week to remember how they lived when God rescued them from Egypt (way back in the book of Exodus). Now the people had returned from exile in Babylon, it was time to thank God in a big way again.

▶ How whole-heartedly did the people celebrate? (v17)

▶ What was the focus of their joy? (v18)

▶ Does it look as if the people are changing for the better?

It must have been an amazing sight! Everyone built these wooden shelters and lived in them for a week. They continued listening to Ezra reading God's word and they held a great feast, celebrating God's goodness to them. They really wanted to start living God's way again. Obeying Him.

GET ON WITH IT

▶ How can you take God's word more seriously?

▶ Which of God's commands do you tend to ignore?

▶ What will you do to sort that out?

PRAY ABOUT IT

Ask God to help you dig deeper into the Bible, learning from Him. And talk to Him about the teaching that you find hardest to obey.

➔ **TAKE IT FURTHER**

Take the branch line to page 115.

40 History lesson

Party's over. The people gather again to hear God's word, but this time the mood is definitely more sombre.

◉ Read Nehemiah 9 v 1–21

ENGAGE YOUR BRAIN

▷ What are the people wearing? (v1)

▷ What do you think that signifies?

▷ What do they do? (v2–3)

▷ What has God done for the Israelites so far in history?
v6:
v7–8:
v9–12:
v13–14:
v15:
v17, 19:
v20–21:

▷ What word would you use to describe the Israelites in these verses?

▷ How about God?

As we'll see in the next part of chapter 9, the people's consistent unfaithfulness is met by God's consistent faithfulness. Our sin is met by God's grace.

THINK IT OVER

▷ How much did the Israelites have to thank God for?

▷ How about us?

▷ But how do we usually respond to God?

PRAY ABOUT IT

Think over the last week, or even the last 24 hours. Spend some time now talking to Him about the times you've failed to go His way, and thank Him for His great mercy in Jesus Christ.

THE BOTTOM LINE

God is good; we reject Him, but still He shows mercy.

→ TAKE IT FURTHER

There's more to learn on page 115.

41 | God is great!

The sorry story goes on. Yet more grace from God thrown back in His face by His ungrateful people.

👁 **Read Nehemiah 9 v 22–37**

ENGAGE YOUR BRAIN

▶ What had God done for His people?
v22–25:
v27b:
v28b:
v30–31:

▶ How did the people respond? (v26, 28–30)

▶ How does v33 sum up all that took place in Israel's history?

▶ What have the people realised by this point?

▶ Do you think they will change?

▶ Why / why not?

▶ How does v26 point to the worst thing God's people will do in the future?

▶ What words are used to describe God throughout chapter 9?

God acts faithfully, while we do wrong. The worst thing human beings ever did was to murder God's Son. But incredibly God used that very act to bring about forgiveness and reconciliation for His enemies. God is so gracious and merciful!

PRAY ABOUT IT

Think about the blessings God has given you. Check out **Ephesians 1 v 3–14** if you need ideas. Thank Him that all of these blessings come because of what Jesus did, not because of what you have done (or failed to do)!

THE BOTTOM LINE

God is faithful; we are not.

→ TAKE IT FURTHER

More amazing words on page 115.

51

42 | Promising future

It's a serious business making promises to God, but that's what the people decide to do. But what exactly are they promising?

Read Nehemiah 9v38–10v39

ENGAGE YOUR BRAIN

▷ What did the people decide to do? (9 v 38)

▷ Who is included in this oath? (10 v 1–28)

▷ What will happen to them if they fail to keep their oath? (v29)

▷ Do you think they will succeed, based on their track record?

▷ What are the three key elements of their oath?
v30:
v31:
v39:

▷ Why do you think those three things are so important?

▷ What does "not neglecting the house of God" involve? (v32–39)

Keeping away from the surrounding nations in marriage, keeping the Sabbath free from trading and money making, and making sure they don't neglect the temple were all things they'd got wrong in the past. But why were they so important? They all boil down to putting God first — not romance, money or self-centredness.

PRAY ABOUT IT

▷ How are you at putting God first?
▷ Is your boyfriend/girlfriend, job, party lifestyle or academic success more important to you?
▷ How do you spend most of your time? Money? Thoughts?

Talk to God about that now and ask Him to show you how amazing Jesus is so that you love Him above everything else.

THE BOTTOM LINE

Put God first.

→ TAKE IT FURTHER

Find a little bit more on page 115.

43 | On the move

Remember Operation Repopulation back in chapter 7? Well, it's about to kick in properly. Not much point in having a rebuilt city with no one living there!

Read Nehemiah v 1–2

ENGAGE YOUR BRAIN

▶ How do the people decide who is to live in Jerusalem? (v1)

▶ How many people will be chosen? (v1)

▶ Sound familiar?

The idea of giving a tenth of something to the Lord (or in this case "the holy city") is called a tithe. It was a way of reminding the people that everything they had, even themselves, belonged to the Lord, and so they would give part of it back to Him.

GET ON WITH IT

The New Testament doesn't tell us we have to give 10% of our time or money to God — instead it tells us to be generous. How can you remind yourself that everything you have is a gift from God by giving of yourself and what you have generously today?

Skim through verses 3–36

▶ Why do you think it's important to have these lists of names?

▶ Where do Judah and Perez (v4) crop up again? (Hint: see Matthew 1 v 3 and 16)

▶ The city is rebuilt. Does it look as though the people are reformed?

PRAY ABOUT IT

There is a story behind all these names — God is still keeping His promises to His people. Thank God that His rescue in Jesus was planned before the foundation of the world.

TAKE IT FURTHER

Move on to page 115.

3 THESE ARE THE PROVINCIAL LEADERS WHO SETTLED IN JERUSALEM (NOW SOME ISRAELI PRIESTS, LEVITES, TEMPLE SERVANTS AND DESCENDANTS OF SOLOMON'S SERVANTS LIVED IN THE TOWNS OF JUDAH, EACH ON THEIR OWN PROPERTY IN THE VARIOUS TOWNS...

Celebration nation

Party time! The walls are up; the people have moved in; everything is looking great! Time to dedicate the walls. And yes, there's another list, but stick with it! It's worth it.

👁 Read Nehemiah 12 v 1–30

The priests and Levites looked after God's temple, offered sacrifices to Him, taught God's Law to the people and led them in worshipping God. The Lord had chosen them to do important stuff — so they got their own list!

ENGAGE YOUR BRAIN

▷ What did they do here? (v24, 27, 30)

▷ Who had originally arranged this method of praising God? (v24)

▷ Does it look as if the people of God are back to the glory days of David & Solomon's kingship?

▷ Why is it so important that the priests, the people and the city are pure? (v30)

▷ Can you remember how God's people are made pure? (eg: Numbers 19 v 1–10)

It's looking promising, but as we'll see in the very next chapter, these positive signs are short lived.

PRAY ABOUT IT

The people of God had to be purified from sin again and again. Thank God that in Jesus we have a great High Priest who has purified us from sin and is sitting at God's right hand (Hebrews 1 v 3).

THE BOTTOM LINE

One day God's people and God's city will be totally free from sin. Thanks to Jesus.

→ TAKE IT FURTHER

Join the party on page 116.

THESE WERE THE PRIESTS AND LEVITES WHO RETURNED WITH ZERUBBABEL SON OF SHEALTIEL AND WITH JOSHUA; SERAIAH, JEREMIAH, EZRA, AMARIAH, MALLUK, HATTUSH, SHEKANIAH, REHUM, MEREMOTH, IDDO,

Praise party

It's a major celebration — two choirs and bands circling the city walls in opposite directions, then arriving at the temple for a huge praise party.

Read Nehemiah 12 v 31–43

ENGAGE YOUR BRAIN

▶ What was the purpose of the two choirs? (v31)

▶ What instruments did they have?

▶ Who was in charge of each choir? (v36, 38)

▶ Where did they stop? (v39)

▶ What happened in the temple? (v43)

▶ Why?

▶ How big were the celebrations? (v43)

Remember how pitiful things looked back in chapter 1 v 3? Now there was definitely cause for rejoicing and God had clearly been at work in all the construction work, even in the face of enemy opposition.

PRAY ABOUT IT

When you pray, do you take time to thank God for all he's done? Or does it turn into a shopping list of all your needs and worries? God tells us to cast all our anxieties on Him, so it's not wrong to pray about those things, but sometimes it's good just to spend time thanking and praising Him. Why not do that right now?

THE BOTTOM LINE

God is worthy of our praise.

TAKE IT FURTHER

Raise the praise on page 116.

46 | Time to change

The Israelites have been marching around Jerusalem, singing and praising God in one massive celebration. They wanted to serve God all the time, but realised that they'd have to make some changes to the way they lived.

Read Nehemiah 12 v 44–47

ENGAGE YOUR BRAIN

▷ Who is provided for? (v44)

▷ What do the Israelites do to make sure God's praise continues to be sung? (v46-47)

▷ Who contributes? (v47)

Read Nehemiah 13 v 1–3

▷ What issue does the reading of the Law highlight? (v1)

▷ Is this just xenophobia (fear of foreigners) or is there a good reason? (v2)

▷ Do the people obey God's word? (v3)

Remember those big three areas the people made oaths about in chapter 10? Keeping away from the surrounding nations in marriage, keeping the Sabbath free from trading and money making,

and making sure they don't neglect the temple. So far it looks as if they're standing by their promises.

THINK IT OVER

Is your faith sometimes all talk and no action? James says: "Faith without deeds is dead" (James 2 v 26). He doesn't mean that doing good things can save us, but if our so-called faith doesn't change the way we live, it was never real to begin with.

PRAY ABOUT IT

Talk to God about how you can put your faith into action this week.

THE BOTTOM LINE

Worship God in word and deed.

➔ TAKE IT FURTHER

More on page 116.

47 | Trouble in store

After such a great celebration comes the fall out.
The city is rebuilt but the people haven't changed.

👁 Read Nehemiah 13 v 4–14

ENGAGE YOUR BRAIN

▶ Why is Eliashib not a great choice to put in charge of the temple storerooms? (v4)

▶ Remember Tobiah? Look back at 6 v 17–19.

▶ What had Eliashib done for Tobiah? (v5) Good idea?

▶ Why was Nehemiah out of the loop? (v6)

▶ What does he do when he finds out? (v7–9)

▶ What else has gone wrong during Nehemiah's absence? (v10)

▶ How does Nehemiah sort the problem out? (v11–13)

▶ What does Nehemiah say to God in response to all of this? (v14)

It hadn't taken long for God's people to go back to their old ways, forgetting God. And there's worse to come. Poor Nehemiah must have felt all his hard work was for nothing, but instead of indulging in self-pity he turns to God. It is God's assessment of our lives that matters.

PRAY ABOUT IT

Ask God to help you to live all out for Him, and for His opinion to be the one that matters most to you.

THE BOTTOM LINE

God's assessment of our lives is the only one that matters.

→ TAKE IT FURTHER

More thoughts have been stored up on page 116.

48 Trouble and strife

As the book of Nehemiah reaches it's climax, things have gone from bad to worse. The city is rebuilt but the people are not reformed. They have fallen back into the same old sins. Is there any hope at all?

👁 Read Nehemiah 13 v 15–31

ENGAGE YOUR BRAIN

- ▶ What is going wrong in v15–16?
- ▶ Why is this such an issue? (v18)
- ▶ What practical steps does Nehemiah take? (v19–22)
- ▶ What's the other big problem? (v23)?
- ▶ What has this led to? (v24)
- ▶ Why is this an issue? (v26)

Half-Israelite children who don't speak the language and with one parent who worships a fake god, can't grow up learning about God. Disaster.

GET ON WITH IT

- ▶ Know a Christian who is dating a non-Christian? Maybe even yourself?
- ▶ What does this passage suggest you should do?

ENGAGE YOUR BRAIN

- ▶ Why is v28 the icing on this rotten cake?

- ▶ What did Nehemiah do? (v25, 28, 30–31)
- ▶ Do you think this worked in the long term?
- ▶ Why do you think Nehemiah repeatedly cries out to God for mercy? (v22, 29, 31)

Despite a short-lived return to following the Law and reinstatement of temple worship the way David and Solomon had set it up, the same sins are tripping Israel up once more.

PRAY ABOUT IT

Thank God that we aren't saved by turning over a new leaf or trying our hardest. Jesus lived the perfect life and died our sinful death so we could truly change from the heart.

THE BOTTOM LINE

If anyone is in Christ, they are a new creation.

→ TAKE IT FURTHER

The last word on Nehemiah is on page 116.

49 By the rivers of Babylon

Time for some more psalms. But not all the psalms are happy songs to God. There are some slow, sad songs too. Here's a classic example.

Read Psalm 137

In 586 BC, God's judgment fell on Judah (God's Old Testament people) for her persistent rejection of Him. The Babylonian army trashed Jerusalem ("Zion") and its temple and carried off God's people into exile. (They would eventually return in the time of Ezra and Nehemiah.)

ENGAGE YOUR BRAIN

▶ What had been their experience in Babylon? (v1)

▶ Why was singing happy songs to order impossible? (v2–4)

▶ How important was God's city to the psalm writer? (v5–6)

▶ What was his prayer for Judah's enemies? (v7–9)

This is such a heartfelt song. The writer looked back on this miserable time suffering God's punishment for rejecting Him. In Babylon, God's people realised how terrible it was to be separated from God's presence. They couldn't even pretend to be happy — it was a desperate situation.

Now that they were back, safe in Jerusalem, they wanted God to act in perfect justice against their enemies. It sounds hideous. But the writer is right to cry to God for justice. The language is shocking and revolting. But these appalling words are expressed in the context of faith in God, the perfect Judge. It's down to God who is punished and who is forgiven. We have to leave it to Him.

PRAY ABOUT IT

It's OK to express our sadness and anger when we talk to God. Tell Him what's getting you down. Ask Him to help you react in a way that's not selfish and which honours Him. And pray for justice — leaving it in His perfect hands.

➡ TAKE IT FURTHER

Off to Revelation on page 117.

50 | Confidence in God

This one's a psalm of thanksgiving by King David. Choose which method you'll use to study it. Read the psalm first, then opt for 1, 2 or 3. Make sure you finish with 4. And if you've got the time and energy, you could do them all.

Read Psalm 138

ONE

We're going to let you in on a secret: thanksgiving psalms usually have five elements:

1. **Intro:** a summary of God's help.
2. **Reminder:** describing the situation God rescued him from.
3. **Prayer:** what the writer cried out to God.
4. **Result:** how God answered.
5. **Praise:** a summary, thanking God.

Now work out which bits of the psalm come under these 5 sections.

TWO

List all that the psalm teaches about God, using these questions:

▶ What does it tell us about God's hearing? (v1–3)
▶ What about His action? (v4–6)
▶ What about His purposes? (v7–8)
▶ What does this psalm say about David's example to us?

THREE

Think "So what?" to these statements — work out what the implications are for you.

v1: David praised God with all his heart.

v1: The Bible says other gods don't exist, but recognises people will try to worship something instead of God.

v3: When David called, God answered his prayer.

v6: God distinguishes between the humble and the proud.

v7: David asked God to keep working in him.

FOUR

David thanks the one and only God, who's proved trustworthy to His people. Select one verse from each section (v1–3, v4–6, v7–8) that you want to remember from now on. Tell God your reasons for choosing them. And thank Him.

→ TAKE IT FURTHER

No *Take it further* today.

51 Safe with God

David's under attack from people who hate him. Scared, he stops to remember just how secure he is in God's hands. This psalm is first class — so take it in.

👁 **Read Psalm 139 v 1–12**

ENGAGE YOUR BRAIN

▶ How well does God know David (and all of us)?

▶ What does God know about us? (v2–4)

▶ Where can we hide from God? (v7–12)

▶ What does God do for His people? (v10)

David's not trying to escape from God; he just recognises it would be impossible to do it. God knows everything about us and He's always with us, guiding us, keeping us safe.

👁 **Read verses 13–24**

▶ How does God know us so intimately? (v13–15)

▶ What's astonishing about v16?

▶ How do we know that David is happy with God's control of his life? (v17–18)

▶ What does David get angry about? (v19–22)

▶ Why? (v20)

▶ What's David's prayer at the end? (v23–24)

God knows everything there is to know about us. Instead of distancing Himself from our sinful lives, He holds on to us, guiding us and protecting us. We can try to run away from Him — but that's stupid and pointless. Or we can be like David, trusting in God to lead us through life.

PRAY ABOUT IT
Now read the psalm to God, as if you'd written it yourself.

→ **TAKE IT FURTHER**
Grab some more on page 117.

TOOLBOX

Twisting Scripture

engage wants to encourage you to dive into God's word, learning how to handle it and understand it more. TOOLBOX gives you tips, tools and advice for wrestling with the Bible. This issue, we ask: How do you spot Scripture twisters?

STICK OR TWIST?

It's so important to handle the Bible correctly as Scripture is the way God has chosen to speak *directly* to us. He can speak to us *indirectly* too — through your circumstances, through wise believers, and through the Holy Spirit working in your life.

But when people interpret the Bible to fit their own desires and preconceived ideas, that's when it can get twisted from truth to error. When you change the Bible's objective truth to fit your life, rather than changing your life to fit the Bible, that's when you risk "twisting Scripture".

"Scripture twisting" is what happens when people interpret the Bible to suit their own false beliefs. The apostle Paul confronted members of the Galatian church who were following "a different way".

"I am astonished that you are so quickly deserting the one who called you by the grace of Christ and are turning to a different gospel — which is really no gospel at all. Evidently some people are throwing you into confusion and are trying to pervert the gospel of Christ" (Galatians 1 v 6–7).

TWISTED RELIGION

Sometimes entire belief systems will come from people who "change the truth" If such people organise and begin teaching others their beliefs, we can call them a "cult". Cults have been defined as "a perversion, a distortion of biblical Christianity". At it's core, a cult

rejects the historic teaching of Christ and the Christian church.

Think about counterfeit money. Convincing fake money looks exactly like the real thing. Experts learn to tell apart counterfeit money, not by studying the fakes (there are too many variations to keep track). They study the real thing (there's only one). People who work in banks are pretty good at recognising counterfeit money because they handle cash all day long.

If you want to get good at spotting false teaching — if you want to develop your spiritual discernment — then spend time with the real deal. Set aside times to regularly study God's word. Get books to help you. Meet with other Christians to dig into and discuss the Bible. Make sure you're handling Scripture every day.

"Do your best to present yourself to God as one approved, a workman who does not need to be ashamed and who correctly handles the word of truth" (2 Timothy 2 v 15).

Learn to handle God's true word correctly, so you're not fooled by fakes, and so you can teach and encourage others.

1 Chronicles

Walk this way

**The Chronicles of Narnia /
The Spiderwick Chronicles /
The Gangster Chronicles etc...
You know the score, you've seen
the word before; it means the
records or history of somewhere
or someone.**

So what or who are these chronicles
chronicling? Well, 1 and 2 Chronicles
focus on Israel's kings — mostly David
and Solomon.

Hang on a minute — didn't we read
all about them in 1 & 2 Samuel and
1 Kings? Isn't this just a re-run? Well,
yes and no. The writer's big focus is
the promise God makes to David.
So a large part of 1 & 2 Chronicles
deal with what God's king should be
like and the temple that God's king
will build for Him. If you're already
familiar with David and Solomon
you'll notice that some episodes are
missed out and others are highlighted
by the writer of Chronicles.

So, was the Chronicler a major royalty
fan then? Maybe, but the glory days
of David and Solomon were long
gone when he was writing 1 & 2
Chronicles. God's people (mostly
Judah — the rest of the tribes had
been scattered by Assyria & Babylon)
were back in their land after exile but
things were in a sorry state. No real
king and only puppet rulers. A fairly
mediocre temple (Ezra 3 v 12). But
God's promises never fail and that's
why the writer puts the focus back on
God's promises to David.

Tied up with all of that is the bigger
picture of whether Israel will walk
God's way or whether they will
ignore and disobey Him. It was still
a problem for the people reading
Chronicles, as it is for us today.

**So, in the red corner we have
God's unfailing promises and
in the blue corner, His people
messing things up. How God will
sort that out is the story of the
whole Bible. So let's see what
1 Chronicles has to say...**

52 | Royal record

Remember those big chunky phone directories? You know, BTI, Before The Internet. The first few chapters of 1 Chronicles can feel a bit like reading the phone book, but these names aren't random.

👁 **Skim read 1 Chronicles 1–3**

▶ Grab a pencil and underline any of the names you recognise.

▶ Who starts the list (1 v 1)?

▶ Who are some of the big names? (1 v 28; 2 v 1–2; 2 v 13–15; 3 v 4–5, 3 v 10–24)

▶ What's so important about these guys?

There are a lot of names here! But the names we're searching for are names in a certain family line, a family that God has made promises to — from Adam, through Noah, Abraham, Isaac, Jacob and Judah to David and Solomon. Big promises. Promises to restore what went wrong in the Garden of Eden. Promises of restored relationship, and a place to live in God's presence for ever under His perfect King.

▶ Why do you think the writer of 1 Chronicles wanted to focus on the royal line even after Jehoiachin was taken captive and God's people were exiled?

▶ What do all these names remind us about God and His promises?

PRAY ABOUT IT

When things are rubbish, do you look at your circumstances or your Saviour? Spend some time thanking God for His promises to you and the way He guarantees them all in Christ.

THE BOTTOM LINE

God is the same yesterday, today and for ever. He always keeps His promises.

➔ **TAKE IT FURTHER**

The lowdown on Chronicles is on page 118.

53 | Prayer of pain

Yesterday we looked at the family line that received God's promises — from Adam and Abraham all the way to David, Solomon and beyond. Today we take a look at how God's people originally settled in the promised land.

Read 1 Chronicles 4 v 1–23

ENGAGE YOUR BRAIN

▶ Which tribe does this section focus on? (v1)

▶ Who gets a special mention in v9–10?

▶ What does his name mean?

Think some celebrities choose weird names for their kids? This poor guy was called Pain. Imagine introducing yourself: "Hello, I'm Agony Smith".

▶ What was notable about Jabez?

▶ Who does he go to for help?

▶ Who does he recognise is the One who controls his destiny?

▶ How does God respond to his prayer?

Some people make a big deal out of this prayer in v10. They reckon we can all pray it today and God will definitely answer it. But the Bible doesn't guarantee this at all; in fact, if you look at Jesus' life on earth, He certainly wasn't kept free from harm and pain. He tells us to "take up your cross and follow me".

The Christian life will include pain and hard times. But God is in control, looking after us. And one day, believers will live with Jesus in an eternity free from pain and suffering.

THE BOTTOM LINE
God doesn't promise us an easy life now, but He guarantees a perfect future.

→ TAKE IT FURTHER
Don't be a pain; turn to page 118.

Entering the promised land

The history lesson continues. And if you don't like history, listen up anyway. This is important stuff about what happened when the promised land was originally settled; some good, some not so good.

Read 1 Chronicles 4 v 24–43

ENGAGE YOUR BRAIN

▶ What are we told about the Simeonites? (v38–43)

▶ Who do they drive out of the land? (v40, 43)

▶ What is the land they inherit like?

God had promised His people a wonderful place to live, and they got it (for a while anyway). But the people who lived there were still sinners and that was obvious from the start.

Read 1 Chronicles 5 v 1–26

▶ What should Reuben and his descendants have expected? (v1)

▶ Why didn't they get it?

▶ Who got it instead?

▶ What are we reminded of about Judah and his descendants? (v2)

▶ What did the Reubenites and Gadites get right? (v20–22)

▶ What was the half-tribe of Manasseh like? (v24)

▶ But what was their big problem? (v25)

▶ How did God deal with them? (v26)

You can be big, strong, successful, brave and famous, but if you're not following God, forget it.

PRAY ABOUT IT

Do you rely on your achievements to feel good about yourself? Remind yourself of Paul's words in **1 Timothy 1 v 15**. Thank God that He loves and accepts you because of Jesus' perfect sacrifice and nothing else. Ask for His strength to keep trusting and following Christ.

THE BOTTOM LINE

Trust in God alone.

→ TAKE IT FURTHER

Controversial foreign policy on page 118.

67

55 The best inheritance

The focus now shifts to the Levites, the descendants of Levi — they get a whole massive chapter to themselves. Why? Read on to find out.

Skim read 1 Chronicles 6

ENGAGE YOUR BRAIN

▷ What is the key thing the Levites did? (v48–49)

▷ Why did God's people need to make atonement?

▷ Any idea what "atonement" means?

God's people were far from holy, but God is totally holy. Bit of a problem there. The only way that sinful people could come close to and be in relationship with the holy God was if their sins were dealt with first. That's why the sacrifices and burnt offerings were needed — then they could be "at one" with God. The word "at-one-ment" was specially invented in the English language to describe this process. Simple.

▷ The Levites didn't get any land of their own — what did they get instead? (v54–81)

▷ Why do you think that was? (See Deuteronomy 10 v 8–9)

Just in case God's people were tempted to think that the physical land of Israel was IT and that they had arrived, the Levites are a reminder that God is their ultimate goal and inheritance.

PRAY ABOUT IT

What are you looking forward to most when Jesus comes back? No more dying, sickness, sorrow or pain? Seeing loved ones again? A perfect world? These are all just the icing on the cake. Thank God that our ultimate goal is being with Jesus. Reflect on the wonder of 1 Corinthians 13 v 12.

THE BOTTOM LINE

God is our inheritance.

TAKE IT FURTHER

Focus on Jesus — page 118.

56 Family planning

More family history to whizz through in these next three chapters, but the focus is narrowing in on a certain man from the tribe of Benjamin (more on him tomorrow).

👁 Read 1 Chronicles 7

▷ What criteria are used to number the descendants of each tribe in chapter 7?

▷ Why do you think that is?

The conquest of Canaan wasn't a walk in the park — God's people had to be ready to fight. The Old Testament book of Numbers makes the same point.

👁 Read 1 Chronicles 8 & 9

▷ Spot any big names? (eg: 8 v 33)

▷ What are we reminded of in the second part of 9 v 1?

▷ But what else are we to remember? (v2)

▷ What does that tell us about God's response to sin?

▷ What does that tell us about God's faithfulness to His promises and His people?

PRAY ABOUT IT

Talk to God about the times when you are unfaithful — ask Him to forgive you. Thank Him that because of Jesus' death and resurrection, we can be totally confident that He loves us and has a future for us.

THE BOTTOM LINE

God never changes.

→ TAKE IT FURTHER

Plan ahead and go to page119.

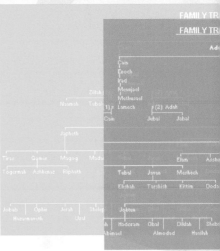

57 | Saul strikes out

We're still thinking about God's promises and one of them was for a king to rule God's people perfectly. The first contender for the role is Saul.

Read 1 Chronicles 9 v 35–44

And then 10 v 1–6

ENGAGE YOUR BRAIN

▶ Look back at 5 v 2 — which line would God's promised ruler come from?

▶ Look at 8 v 33 and 8 v 40. What line was Saul descended from?

▶ How does Saul meet his end? (10 v 1–6)

Israel's first king came to a pretty sorry end. Defeated in battle by the enemies of God's people, the Philistines, he killed himself rather than fight on until God decided his life should end.

Read verses 7–14

▶ What about Saul's behaviour clearly showed he was not God's promised king? (v13–14)

▶ Who does God give the throne to instead (v14)?

Saul failed to trust God — he didn't follow God's instructions, and even when things went terribly wrong, he refused to turn back to the Lord for guidance. So God handed him over to his enemies.

PRAY ABOUT IT

We can all be like Saul — thinking we know better than God, refusing to go His way. Look at the only person who trusted His Heavenly Father when it looked crazy, and obeyed Him perfectly even to death. Read **Matthew 26 v 36–46** and talk to God about it.

→ TAKE IT FURTHER

Find strength on page 119.

58 | David steps forward

Israel's second king is quite a contrast to Saul.
Saul was unfaithful and abandoned: David is
faithful and blessed.

👁 **Read 1 Chronicles 11 v 1–3**

ENGAGE YOUR BRAIN

▷ How do the ordinary Israelites feel
about David? (v1–2)

▷ What word does God use to
describe the sort of king David
will be? (v2)

▷ What does that suggest to you?

▷ Does God's promise come true?
(v3)

God's people need a shepherd
because they are like sheep —
defenceless, a bit dim and prone
to wandering off!

👁 **Read verses 4–9**

▷ What does David do as king?
v4–5:
v7:
v8:

▷ Why is he so successful? (v9)

God's promises always come true; He
is utterly reliable. And when the Lord
is with you, nothing can stop you!

PRAY ABOUT IT
Two verses to think about as you
pray about today's passage:
Matthew 1 v 23 and
Romans 8 v 31.

THE BOTTOM LINE
The Lord is MY shepherd.

➔ TAKE IT FURTHER
Go sheepishly to page 119.

71

59 Mighty men

The next part of Chronicles sounds like an action movie. Forget The Avengers — David's mighty men could give any superhero a run for their money!

👁 **Read 1 Chronicles 11 v 10–47**

ENGAGE YOUR BRAIN

▷ *What was so great about "The Three"? (v11–19)*

▷ *What about Abishai? (v20–21)*

▷ *And Benaiah? (v22–25)*

▷ *What are we reminded about throughout this chapter? (v10, 14)*

David has some seriously impressive warriors in his army, but sadly one of the most devoted will meet a tragic end. Uriah (v41) is incredibly loyal to David but David repays him by sleeping with his wife and then having him murdered. Sad times.

However great David was, and he was pretty awesome, he was not perfect. In fact he was a sinner like us (Psalm 51 v 5). Thank God that in Jesus we have the perfect King who not only is totally sinless but also died so that we (and David) could be forgiven.

PRAY ABOUT IT

Why not make Psalm 51 your own prayer now?

THE BOTTOM LINE

Even the mightiest of us is a sinner who needs Jesus.

→ TAKE IT FURTHER

More about mighty men on p119.

For a brilliant book on David's mighty men, check out The Hard Corps *by Dai Hankey.* You can find it at *www.thegoodbook.co.uk*

Join in!

Once a runaway fugitive from King Saul, David becomes the massively popular new king. How? The loyal support of literally hundreds of fighting men? Yes, but that's not the whole story...

👁 **Skim read 1 Chronicles 12**

ENGAGE YOUR BRAIN

▶ *Who joined David while he was on the run from Saul? (v1–7)*

▶ *Who later joins David's crew? (v8)*

▶ *How brave are they?*

▶ *What is David worried about as more men join him? (v17)*

▶ *What do all these men have in common?*

▶ *How united are they? (v38–40)*

▶ *What truth had they grasped? (v18)*

▶ *Who is ultimately the one making David king?*

The Archbishop of Canterbury once said: "Find out what God is doing and join in", and that's exactly what is happening here. God has said He will make David king and the rest of Israel is gradually falling in with His plans!

👁 **Read Matthew 28 v 18–20**

GET ON WITH IT

▶ *How can you get involved with what God is doing today?*

PRAY ABOUT IT

The Bible tells us that God's ultimate aim is to bring everything under Jesus' rule (Ephesians 1 v 9–10). Thank God that He has given His people the wonderful job of sharing the good news about Jesus with others so that they can know Him as their king. Pray for a chance to do that today.

THE BOTTOM LINE

God is at work. Join in!

→ **TAKE IT FURTHER**

Join in the fun on page 119.

61 | Ark and ride

The Ark was where God's presence on earth rested. It was supposed to be at the heart of the tabernacle — the tent of meeting where God would come close to His people after the priests had offered the correct sacrifices for sin.

But under Saul's rule, God's guidance was ignored and the ark was forgotten. Remind yourself of where Saul sought answers rather than going to God (1 Chronicles 10 v 13).

▣ Read 1 Chronicles 13 v 1–14

ENGAGE YOUR BRAIN

▣ *What is David's plan? (v1–4)*

▣ *Why does he want to do this? (v3)*

▣ *How do David and the people set about bringing the Ark back?*

▣ *What is the national mood (v8)?*

▣ *Why does that suddenly change? (v10)*

▣ *How does David respond? (v11–13)*

▣ *Why do you think he feels this way?*

▣ *Do you think he makes a good decision?*

▣ *What happens to Obed-Edom's house while the Ark is there?*

It was done with the best of intentions, but it wasn't done God's way. The ark was far too holy for just anyone to get close to. Thankfully, through Jesus we have free access to our holy and powerful God, but don't make the mistake of taking that access for granted.

PRAY ABOUT IT

Say sorry to God now for the times when you've taken for granted the privilege of being able to be close to Him. Thank Him for all that Jesus did to make it possible.

→ TAKE IT FURTHER

Take a trip to Narnia on page 120.

2 & 3 John

Sure signs

We're now going to delve into two books that often get ignored. They're both short letters written by John, one of Jesus' twelve disciples. He also wrote John's Gospel and Revelation. And of course, he wrote the letter "1 John". These two shorter letters are like summaries of the stuff covered in that longer letter.

Here, John reminds his readers that...
• Jesus really is God's Son, who became human
• we should obey God
• we must love God's people
• we need to watch out for false teaching.

2 JOHN

This letter was written to urge Christians to care for each other and to warn them about false teachers (like the conmen referred to in 1 John). How should these Christians react to wrong teaching — and also, importantly, to those who taught it? And how should we react?

3 JOHN

Was written to a man called Gaius, to urge him to carry on welcoming good Christian teachers. And to warn him about the damage that a negative leader could do to a church. And to hold onto both truth and love, which is something we all need to do.

These letters may be small, but ask God to use them to have a BIG impact on your life.

62 | Truth and love

Times were changing for Christians at the end of the first century AD. The apostles — who saw Jesus risen from the dead and passed on the truth about Him — were dying out.

In their place were lots of travelling preachers. Some of them claimed to have totally new teaching, beyond what the apostles said. Others called for a return to Jewish ways. Who should the churches believe? Crucially, how would they remain strong in faith. And how about us?

Read 2 John v 1–4

ENGAGE YOUR BRAIN
- What does John call himself? (v1)
- What links all of God's people? (v1–2)
- What does God give all believers?
- What should give us real joy? (v4)

"The chosen lady" (v1) probably refers to the specific church John was writing to, with "her children" being the church members. John was happy to hear that many people in the church were walking God's way.

THINK IT OVER
- Are you happy when you see other Christians really going for it in the Christian life?
- Do you ever let jealousy get in the way?
- Who can you encourage today?

Christians have a special bond and love each other because of the truth we share. The truth that Jesus died for us to rescue us and forgive us. He has shown unbeatable love to us, so we should show love to each other.

GET ON WITH IT
Pick three Christians you know. Send a message to each of them, using the stuff mentioned in v3.

THE BOTTOM LINE
Grace, mercy and peace from God... will be with us in truth and love.

→ TAKE IT FURTHER
Face the truth on page 120.

63 Love life

Try describing LOVE in one sentence:

👁 **Read 2 John v 5–6**

ENGAGE YOUR BRAIN

▶ *What old command does John say is crucial? (v5)*

▶ *How does John define love?*

▶ *How does that differ from your definition of love?*

▶ *What does God expect from us?*

Love is vital to the Christian life. Love for God and showing love to each other. Because real love is obeying God — living His way. If we do that, we'll be loving to others along the way. The more we obey God, the more our lives will be filled with love.

👁 **Read John 14 v 15–24**

▶ *How do Jesus' followers show their love for Him? (v15)*

▶ *What brilliant promise did Jesus make? (v16–17)*

▶ *What else is true for believers? (v21)*

Jesus' followers (Christians) show their love for Him by obeying Him. That's easier said than done. But He's not left us to do it on our own. Jesus has given His Spirit to every believer. The Holy Spirit strengthens and encourages Christians, enabling them to obey Jesus.

GET ON WITH IT

▶ *What specific action do you need to take?*

PRAY ABOUT IT

Ask God to help you obey His commands, so that His love shines through in the way that you live.

THE BOTTOM LINE

Love one another. Obey God's commands.

→ **TAKE IT FURTHER**

More love advice from John can be found on page 120.

64 | Watch out!

John now turns his attention to false teachers.
These people were persuasively teaching lies about
Jesus and were leading people away from God.
John says: "Watch out!"

Read 2 John v 7–11

ENGAGE YOUR BRAIN

- ▶ What basic fact did these men get wrong?
- ▶ What does John call them? (v7)
- ▶ What's his warning to the church? (v8)
- ▶ Can you know God without trusting in Jesus? (v9)
- ▶ How should we treat people who teach weird stuff about Jesus? (v10)
- ▶ What's true for people who welcome false teachers? (v11)

Anyone who claims Jesus wasn't real or wasn't human or isn't really God... is a deceiver and we shouldn't listen to them. Such people can often be very subtle. We need to check that anyone who influences is saying stuff that agrees with the Bible. Otherwise we'll be led away from Jesus.

And watch out for people who claim you can know God but don't need Jesus. Or that all religions lead to God. Trusting in Jesus Christ and His death in our place is essential to getting to know God. Without Jesus, we have nothing.

THINK IT OVER

- ▶ How do you react when you hear false claims about Christianity?
- ▶ How should you react?
- ▶ How can you stand up more for your faith in Jesus?

Read verses 12–13

- ▶ How does John want to encourage these Christians?
- ▶ How else does he encourage them?
- ▶ Who will you meet up with to encourage?

PRAY ABOUT IT

Talk to God about anything that's on your mind today. Ask Him to help you not be swayed by false teaching.

→ TAKE IT FURTHER

Watch out for more on page 120.

65 | Spiritual health

Here's another mini-letter from John, "the elder". This one is written to his friend Gaius. Like the last letter, John has a dig at people who were getting in the way of the gospel. But first, he gives loads of encouragement.

👁 **Read 3 John v 1–2**

ENGAGE YOUR BRAIN

▶ How is Gaius described? (v1)

▶ What does John pray for him? (v2)

PRAY ABOUT IT

John prays for his friend's physical health and spiritual health. Take time now to pray for at least two Christian friends, praying for both their physical and spiritual health.

👁 **Read verses 3–4**

▶ What put a smile on John's face?

▶ What do you think it means to be "faithful to the truth"?

John knew that Gaius was spiritually healthy because other Christians had told him how Gaius was getting along. They saw that his life was full of God's truth and that he walked God's way. He not only believed the truth about Jesus — he let it affect every area of his life.

THINK IT OVER

▶ Do you believe in Jesus?

▶ So how does it affect your life?

▶ In what areas do you need to "walk in truth" more?

PRAY ABOUT IT

Ask God to make you spiritually healthy, so that the truth of the gospel impacts every area of your life.

THE BOTTOM LINE

Walk in the truth.

→ TAKE IT FURTHER

Extra time to pray, as there's no *Take it further* section today.

66 | Serving suggestion

Yesterday, we met "spiritually healthy" Gaius.
Today, we learn from him what it means to walk God's
way and how we can do this in a very practical way.

👁 Read 3 John v 5–8

ENGAGE YOUR BRAIN

▷ How did Gaius' love stand out?
(v5)

▷ What does John encourage him
to do? (v6)

▷ Any idea why these guys were
travelling around? (v7)

▷ How should we treat such gospel
workers? (v8)

These men were missionaries,
travelling from city to city, telling
people about Jesus ("the Name").
That's why Gaius looked after them
even though they were strangers.
And we should do the same —
welcoming and supporting anyone
who spreads the message of Jesus.

GET ON WITH IT

▷ How can you support gospel
workers?
  • give money to missionaries?

• treat a penniless Christian
worker to a meal?
• send them encouraging
messages?
• pray for them?

Now write exactly what you'll
do, so that you do it:

PRAY ABOUT IT

Spend time praying for Christian
workers you know. And ask God to
help you do whatever you've written
in the box.

➡ TAKE IT FURTHER

First, serve – page 121.

67 | Spot the difference

We've heard all about godly Gaius.
Now we meet dire Diotrephes.

👁 **Read 3 John v 9–14**

ENGAGE YOUR BRAIN

▶ What was scandalous about this guy's attitude? (v9–10)

▶ What was John's plan to solve the crisis? (v9–10)

▶ What does John urge Gaius to do? (v11)

▶ How does he divide people into two groups? (v11)

▶ Who is held up as a good example? (v12)

▶ How does John end his letter? (v13–14)

THINK IT THROUGH

▶ Are you ever like Diotrephes, putting yourself first?

▶ Who was the last person you gossiped about maliciously?

▶ Any Christians you're not friendly or welcoming towards?

GET ON WITH IT

▶ What evil do you need to stop imitating?

▶ Which Christians do you look up to?

▶ What godly characteristic of theirs can you imitate?

▶ Anything you feel you should do this week, so you start walking God's way more?

PRAY ABOUT IT

Read through the *Think it over and Get on with it* sections again, talking to God about anything He's challenged or encouraged you with. Ask for His help to live His way.

→ **TAKE IT FURTHER**

A little bit more on page 121.

Why go to church?

Everyone has had different experiences of church. For some of us, it feels like home — we meet our friends there and grow in our faith. For others, church is deadly dull or just full of old people you can't relate to. Some of us have had brilliant experiences of church, and some of us have had terrible experiences that have put us off for life. So, do Christians really need to go to church?

FAMILY HOME

"I don't want to go to church. The music is rubbish. Nobody ever speaks to me. There are no teenagers except Billy and he's really weird."

"Going to church doesn't make you a Christian, right? So I'll just carry on by myself — God knows what's in my heart."

This might be your situation, or maybe your church is full of teenagers with a big youth group, great music and friendly church members who take a real interest in you.

But church isn't an optional activity for Christians. Just substitute the word "church" for a minute with "God's family". Perhaps in your moodier moments you might not want to be associated with your embarrassing dad, bossy mum and frankly annoying brother, but like it or not, they are your family! And like it or not, every Christian is a member of God's family, and what's not to like about that?

ESSENTIAL ENCOURAGEMENT

Here's what the Bible says about meeting with God's family (not just "going to church"):

"Let us hold unswervingly to the hope we profess, for he who promised is faithful. And let us consider how we

may spur one another on towards love and good deeds. Let us not give up meeting together, as some are in the habit of doing, but let us encourage one another — and all the more as you see the Day approaching" (Hebrews 10 v 23–25)

We need to keep meeting together so we can encourage one another to hold onto our faith, to love and do good deeds so that we are ready for the day when Jesus comes back.

We are not designed to be lonely Christians; it's hard to keep going on our own. If you take a piece of charcoal out of a barbecue, it soon grows cold; stick it back alongside all the other pieces, and it glows with heat again. God has given us each other, so don't throw that gift back in His face by refusing to hang out with your Christian brothers and sisters.

BE BRAVE

If you're stuck in a church like the one Billy goes to, remember God has given you those people. Maybe nobody speaks to you — but do you ever speak to them? It may be hard to believe, but older people can find teenagers a bit intimidating.

Why not start by just saying hello or asking how their week has been? If you're really brave you could ask what they found interesting/challenging/encouraging about the tallk! Perhaps Billy is a bit weird, but God loves him and Jesus died for him... would it hurt to smile at him or even sit next to him? Go on, give it a try!

God has given us a Christian family to help us grow, and for us to help them grow too. Ask Him to help you to see things that way and ask Him (and yourself) what could you do to play your part in your church family? Help with the kids work? Make coffee? Set up chairs? Run the sound desk? And most importantly; just be there.

68 | Proverbs: Living for God

It's that time again. Time to dive back into the weird world of Proverbs. Get ready for more strange sayings. More importantly, prepare yourself for God speaking wise words that could shake your world.

👁 Read Proverbs 21 v 1–10

ENGAGE YOUR BRAIN

▶ What are we told about living God's way? (v2, 3)

▶ Which of these proverbs seems most relevant to you right now?

Verses 5 and 7 don't seem right. Often it's the ungodly people — those who look after number 1 — who do best in life, isn't it? Actually, no. Put these verses in an eternal perspective, in the light of God's judgment. One day, God will put things right. Evil will be punished. Those who love God will live with Him in eternal perfection.

👁 Read verses 11–21

▶ What are we told about doing good? (v15, 21)

▶ And about not doing good? (v13)

▶ Try putting these proverbs into your own words...
v12:

v17:

Read verses 22–31

▶ What advice are we given about what we say? (v23, 24, 28)

▶ What's so brilliantly encouraging about v30–31?

▶ Any other verses here that stand out to you?

Sometimes it seems that it pays to reject God and to live for yourself. But, in the end, people who turn against God will pay the price. Human wisdom and plans can't succeed against the Lord. God WILL win the victory.

PRAY ABOUT IT

Talk to God about anything that's really struck you today. Thank Him that He's in complete control and that nothing can defeat Him.

➔ TAKE IT FURTHER

For a different perspective: page 121.

69 Rich and poor

Would you say you're a generous person? As usual, this section of Proverbs has lots to say on a variety of subjects. But look out for the focus on money.

Read Proverbs 22 v 1–16

ENGAGE YOUR BRAIN

▷ How should v1 change our attitude to success?

▷ What does v2 tell us about wealth?

▷ How do people abuse their wealth? (v7)

▷ What will happen to them? (v16)

▷ But what should God's people do? (v9)

Christians get a good reputation by living God's way and treating people fairly; not by chasing after wealth or misusing it.

THINK IT OVER

▷ How does your attitude to success and wealth need to change?

▷ How will you be generous today/ tomorrow?

Read the chapter again

▷ Which proverbs leap out at you?

▷ Which seem strange to you?

▷ Which one is most relevant to your situation right now?

▷ What steps do you need to take?

PRAY ABOUT IT

Write down some of the implications that proverb has for you. And talk to God about it.

→ TAKE IT FURTHER

Reasons to get generous on page 121.

70 | Wise up

Now we enter a section of Proverbs called "Sayings of the Wise". What's the difference from what we've been reading so far? Well, many of the verses go together, rather than being one-offs. Time to get wise...

👁 **Read Proverbs 22 v 17–21**

ENGAGE YOUR BRAIN

▷ *What are we expected to do as we read Proverbs? (v17)*

▷ *Why?*
  v18:
  v19:
  v21:

There are four steps that will help us read Proverbs.

1. **Listen.** Take the proverb in.
2. **Apply.** Let it affect your life.
3. **Memorise.** Try to remember proverbs that seem important to you.
4. **Quote.** Share the best proverbs with other people.

Doing all of this will help us to trust God more and even enable us teach others. Nice one.

👁 **Read verses 22–29**

Pick one of the proverbs (or pairs of proverbs) here and...

1. **Listen.** Read through it again and take on board what God is saying to you.
2. **Apply.** So what are you gonna do?
3. **Memorise.** Take time to learn it.
4. **Quote.** Now tell someone all about it. (Go on, don't be shy.)

PRAY ABOUT IT
Oops, we missed out step 5: Talk about it with the Lord.

→ TAKE IT FURTHER
Don't follow the crowd... take a diversion to page 121.

Central defender

👁 **Read Proverbs 23 v 1–9**

ENGAGE YOUR BRAIN

▶ *What's the main point from each of these sections?*
v1–3:
v4–5:
v6–8:
v9:

▶ *Does any of them speak directly to you?*

Loads about food here. First up, gluttony — greed. "Put a knife to your throat" means take whatever measures are necessary to stop greed taking over your life. And don't waste your time chasing after money (v4). It's pointless — it won't last. And watch out for penny-pinchers and fools (v6–9).

👁 **Read verses 10–18**

▶ *Anything stand out to you here?*

▶ *So what? How will you make it count?*

Verse 10 talks about messing around with the boundaries of people's land, stealing land from them. If someone defends their rights, you could be in trouble. The Bible describes God as the Defender of His people — loyal and committed to looking after them. Fighting on their side. Remember this whenever you face opposition for being a Christian.

Verses 17–18 contain another gem. Don't get jealous when sinners seem to be doing well. Be enthusiastic about living God's way — because there's an amazing future with God ahead of you!

PRAY ABOUT IT

Ask God to help you get your priorities straight — living for Him, not money or anything else. Thank Him that He's your Defender, winning the victory for you.

→ TAKE IT FURTHER

Defensive formation — 121.

72 | Drunk and disorderly

Today's proverbs talk about alcohol. They don't say:
"Drinking is wrong — stay away!" But they do warn
us of the mess we can get into if we drink too much.

Read Proverbs 23 v 19–28

ENGAGE YOUR BRAIN

▶ *What does the writer want us to do? (v19, 26)*

▶ *What are some of the ways we keep our hearts on the right path?*
v20:
v22:
v23:
v26–28

Read verses 29–35

▶ *What do drunkards look like to others? (v29)*

▶ *How can you turn v31 into a positive piece of advice?*

▶ *What are the warnings for drinking too much?*
v32:
v33:
v34–35:

Drinking alcohol in moderation is fine. But don't be fooled — it's easy to go too far and mess up. The obvious dangers include wasting your money (v21), becoming addicted (v31), impairing your thinking and decision-making (v35). Not to mention being more open to temptation and being a bad witness as a Christian.

THINK IT OVER

▶ *How would you describe your relationship with alcohol?*
▶ *How can you honour God more in this area?*
▶ *What action do you need to take?*
▶ *Got any friends who struggle with booze?*
▶ *How can you be a positive influence on them?*

PRAY ABOUT IT

Only you know what you need to say to God today.

→ TAKE IT FURTHER

Extra alcohol available on page 122.

73 | Words of wisdom

Are you ready for more life-changing proverbs?
Really ready? Have you asked God to challenge
you and and change you through His word? If not,
now's your chance, before we start.

Read Proverbs 24 v 1–22

ENGAGE YOUR BRAIN

Remember, true wisdom is to "fear the Lord" — live God's way.

▷ What do we learn about wisdom here?
v3–4:
v5–7:
v13–14:

▷ And what does God tell us about evil/sin?
v1–2:
v8–9:
v19–20:

Read verses 11–12 again

We can't use the excuse of ignorance to avoid helping people in need.

▷ Is there anyone who could use your help, who you've been ignoring?

▷ So... what will you do?

PRAY ABOUT IT

Use the space below to write out a prayer to God that relates to today's chapter. Take your time, and then read it to God.

→ TAKE IT FURTHER

Check out page 122.

74 Fair enough

We're going to have one last look at Proverbs this issue. These wise sayings focus on fairness and laziness. Don't be a sluggard — read these proverbs, pray about them and act on them.

Read Proverbs 24 v 23–29

ENGAGE YOUR BRAIN

▶ How should we not treat people?
v23:
v28:
v29:

▶ How do people view those who are unfair or abuse their power? (v24)

▶ What about those who are fair? (v25)

▶ How good is honesty? (v27)

If people were truly wise — living God's way — the world would be a much fairer place. God expects those with power (judges, police, politicians, bosses etc) to treat people fairly. But that's not just the responsibility of powerful people; we should all treat others fairly. Don't lie or gossip about people, or twist the truth. And don't seek revenge. Remember, honest words are as good as a kiss!

Read verses 27, 30–34

▶ What do you think v27 means?

▶ What did the writer see at the lazy man's place? (v30–31)

▶ What did he learn from it? (v32–34)

Yet again, Proverbs says: "Don't be lazy — you'll regret it!" Instead, work hard and plan well before doing something big like building a house or starting a family (v27).

GET ON WITH IT
▶ What has God taught you today?

▶ Anything you need to do?

PRAY ABOUT IT
Pray for specific people with power and responsibility. Pray that they would be fair and that they would use their power for God's purposes.

→ TAKE IT FURTHER
Fair's fair on page 122.

75 Desperate situation

How do you react to a crisis? Hard times can easily detach us from God and godly living, can't they? Let's see how King David reacted when under constant attack.

👁 **Read Psalm 140**

ENGAGE YOUR BRAIN

▷ *What is David's prayer? (v1, 4)*

▷ *What are his enemies like? (v1–3)*

▷ *What have they been doing? (v4–5)*

▷ *What truths about God does he hang on to?*
v7:
v12:

▷ *So what does David ask God for? (v8–11)*

You've probably not had an experience quite like David's — surrounded by enemies laying traps for you. But you probably have experienced the hurt caused by sharp tongues and lying lips (v3). When people tear your character to shreds or when gossip leaves you feeling alone and isolated.

Maybe your first thought was revenge. But remember, yesterday we read that vengeance should be left to God and we should treat our enemies with kindness. When harsh words devastate us, we must cling on to what we know about God: His great mercy, His perfect justice and His care for people in need. We can turn to God in times of trouble, knowing He hears our cries and wants to help us.

PRAY ABOUT IT

Pray for any "enemies" you have. Talk to God about any crisis you're facing. Tell Him how you feel. Repent of any thoughts of revenge or any harsh words you've used. Ask God to rescue you and to help you praise Him with the way you live your life (v13).

→ TAKE IT FURTHER

Tongue twisters on page 122.

76 | 1 Chronicles: Walk this way

God's promises just keep on coming true!
And God's king (mostly) lives God's way.

Read 1 Chronicles 14 v 1–17

ENGAGE YOUR BRAIN

▶ What promises about a king has God made in Israel's history? Deuteronomy 17 v 14–20:

Genesis 49 v 10:

▶ Can you see them being fulfilled in chapter 14?

▶ What is good about David? (v2, 10, 14, 16)

▶ What is not so great? (v3)

▶ Why? (See Deuteronomy 17 v 17)

Another reminder that although David is great — he is not the greatest. God invented marriage to be between one man and one woman. When His people deviate from that, it never works out.

▶ Who is behind David's success as a king? (v2, 17)

Rest from enemies, respect from the surrounding nations — these are all fulfilments of God's promises, but the best is yet to come.

PRAY ABOUT IT

Isn't it amazing that when Jesus was crucified, He was still fulfilling these predictions for God's perfect king? He defeated our enemies: sin, death and the devil. And the surrounding nations came to worship Him — a Roman centurion of all people said: "Surely this man was the Son of God". Thank God for Jesus.

THE BOTTOM LINE

Jesus is God's perfect King.

→ TAKE IT FURTHER

More predictions on page 123.

77 | Ark life

Operation Ark Part 2. This time David had learned from his deadly mistakes. Need a reminder of what happened earlier? Then check out chapter 13.

👁 **Read 1 Chronicles 15**

ENGAGE YOUR BRAIN

▶ What has David realised about the ark? (v2, 13)
▶ Who does he gather together? (v3–11)
▶ What does he ask the Levites to do? (v12)
▶ How do they go about moving the Ark? (v15)
▶ Whose rules are they following?

This time David and co stuck by God's rules — they did things His way and He blessed them. Ecclesiastes 12 v 13 tells us: *"Fear God and keep his commandments, for this is the whole duty of man."* Jesus also told His disciples that *"you are my friends if you do what I command"* (John 15 v 14).

PRAY ABOUT IT

It's impossible to keep God's commands in our own strength but Jesus gives us His Holy Spirit to enable us to walk His way.

Ask for His help now.

👁 **Read verses 16–29**

▶ How does God respond this time? (v26)
▶ What is the national mood? (v16, 28)
▶ Is everyone celebrating (v29)?
▶ Why do you think Michal felt this way?

2 Samuel 6 v 16–23 gives more detail about Michal's reaction. She failed to understand that there was only one king's honour at stake here — God's!

GET ON WITH IT

Are you prepared to obey God's commands and honour Him even if other people sneer at you or despise you for it?

THE BOTTOM LINE

Fear God and keep His commands.

➔ TAKE IT FURTHER

Encouraging words from Jesus — page 123.

78 | Thanks, God!

The Ark has arrived and David and his people are partying.

Read 1 Chronicles 16 v 1–22

ENGAGE YOUR BRAIN

▶ What's the first thing they do when the Ark is placed inside its tent? (v1)
▶ Why do you think they do this?
▶ How do they celebrate? (3)

PRAY ABOUT IT

The Levites' job involved making petition (asking for things), giving thanks and praising God. 1 Peter 2 v 9 tells us that Christians are a "royal priesthood" so do those same three things now as you speak to God.

David was a great song writer. Take a look at v8–22 and fill in the table below:

Reasons to praise God	How we should respond to Him

GET ON WITH IT

Go on then! Put v8–12 in action!

TAKE IT FURTHER

Revealing stuff on page 123.

79 | Lasting love

God has brought His Ark (a symbol of Him being with His people) back to Jerusalem. The people are partying and praising God. Here's the second half of David's super psalm (or psuper psalm if you like).

👁 **Read 1 Chronicles 16 v 23–36**

ENGAGE YOUR BRAIN

The first half of David's psalm focused on what God had done for His special people, Israel.

▷ *What about the second half?*

▷ *Who should recognise God's rule? (v24, v28–29)*

▷ *Instead of what? (v26)*

David longs for all of creation — including nations outside of God's chosen people — to come and praise Him.

▷ *When will that happen? (Revelation 7 v 9–12)*

▷ *What else does David say should recognise God's rule? (v23, v30-33)*

▷ *Why can Israel praise God? (v34–36)*

▷ *What can they alone call God?*

PRAY ABOUT IT

If you are a Christian, you can give thanks to the Lord, not only as your Creator and Ruler, but as your Saviour (v35). Spend some time reflecting on that and thanking Him now.

👁 **Read verses 37–43**

▷ *What is all activity at the tabernacle to be based on? (v40)*

▷ *Which of God's characteristics are the Levites to especially remember? (v41)*

THE BOTTOM LINE

Give thanks to the Lord; His love endures forever!

→ TAKE IT FURTHER

A tiny bit more can be found on page 123.

80 | House party

David's doing well for himself — or rather God is doing well for him. He's got a beautiful palace made of top quality materials but God's ark is still living in a tent. This bothered David.

👁 Read 1 Chronicles 17 v 1–6

ENGAGE YOUR BRAIN

▶ What is Nathan the prophet's reaction to David's concern? (v2)

▶ Sound good? What is God's surprising response? (v3–6)

Amazingly, God isn't bothered about having a house built for Him. The whole point about His ark being in a tent (or tabernacle) was that He lived and travelled with His people, in the same surroundings as them.

PRAY ABOUT IT

Read John 1 v 14 — the words "made his dwelling among us" literally mean "tabernacled among us". God hasn't changed the way He relates to His people. He always wanted to get close and be at the centre of their lives. In Jesus He does this in an incredibly close way! Thank God that "the Word became flesh".

👁 Read verses 7–15

God says: "It's not what you can do for me; it's what I will do for you."

▶ What blessings does God promise David in v7–15? List them:

▶ Who do you think v11–14 is talking about?

-
-
-
-
-

In some ways it's easy to say these verses are about Solomon — after all, he was an even more powerful king than his father and he did build a house for God (the temple). But they are even more true of Jesus.

PRAY ABOUT IT

Thank God for sending Jesus as the perfect King in charge of our lives.

→ TAKE IT FURTHER

Make a house call on page 123.

Blessed is best

After such awesome promises from God, what can David say?

👁 **Read 1 Chronicles 17 v 16–27**

THINK ABOUT IT

▢ *What has God done for David? (v16–17)*

▢ *Why does this blow his mind?*

▢ *How does David respond to what God has done and promised to do?*

▢ *What does he acknowledge about God? (v20)*

▢ *What does David recognise about what God has done, not only for him but for his people? (v21–22)*

▢ *Why does David want God's promises to him to come true? (v23–24)*

David's not concerned about his own glory or status — he knows that God's promise-keeping will result in the world realising that God is King!

God's people want everyone to know how great He is.

▢ *What is David most excited by? (v27)*

Being blessed by God ultimately means being "in his sight" for ever. David is under no illusions here — palaces and wealth are all very nice, but it's being in God's presence that brings true and eternal blessedness.

PRAY ABOUT IT

David and you (if you follow Jesus) are blessed by being for ever in His sight. Pray for people now who don't yet trust Jesus, that they would turn to Him before it's too late and they miss out on being with Him for ever.

THE BOTTOM LINE

There is no one like you, O Lord.

➡ **TAKE IT FURTHER**

A glimpse of the future on page 123.

82 God's great king

Chronicles gives us a snapshot of David's time as king. The next few chapters focus mostly on his military successes. So get ready for action.

Read 1 Chronicles 18 v 1–13

ENGAGE YOUR BRAIN

▶ How successful is David's rule in international terms? (v1–13)

▶ Who does he defeat?

▶ What is the outcome of his military victories? (v2, 6, 8, 10)

▶ What does David do with all this stuff? (v11)

▶ What is the reason for David's success? (v6, 13)

No empire building for its own sake here. David is serving God and the Lord is keeping His promises to His people — rest from enemies and material prosperity.

Read verses 14–17

▶ How successful is David's rule at a national level? (v14–17)

▶ Why was he such a good king?

PRAY ABOUT IT

David's rule at its best shows us what Jesus' perfect kingdom will be like. All our enemies will be defeated; we will live in perfect safety; we will have everything we need; and we will be ruled by someone who has our best interests at heart. Spend time now giving thanks for this amazing future for God's people.

→ TAKE IT FURTHER

Meet the King on page 124.

83 | Battle stations

More warfare today and some fairly nasty characters are giving David grief this time.

👁 **Read 1 Chronicles 19 v 1–19**

ENGAGE YOUR BRAIN

▷ What was David's reaction to King Nahash's death? (v2)

▷ How did the Ammonites interpret it? (v3)

▷ And how did they treat David's messengers? (v4)

It sounds funny to us, but it was deeply embarrassing to be treated like that. See how sensitively David treats his humiliated messengers (v5).

▷ What happened when the Ammonites realised their big mistake? (v6–7)

▷ How did David respond? (v8)

▷ And the outcome? (v15–19)

▷ Who was in control? (v13)

👁 **Read 1 Chronicles 20 v 1–8**

▷ What happened to the Ammonites? (v1–4)

▷ And the rest of Israel's enemies? (v5–8)

▷ What had God promised David? (1 Chronicles 17 v 9–10)

OK, so most of us won't be winning military victories for God. Yet God's blessings for His people now — those who, like David, walk God's way — are far better. They're all to be found in Jesus: He assures us we're forgiven by God; brings us into a lasting relationship with God; lives in us by His Spirit; and guarantees us life in God's new world.

PRAY ABOUT IT

Thank God for His willingness to give His people good things. And resolve, with God's help, to walk His way.

⇨ **TAKE IT FURTHER**

Go behind the scenes on page 124.

Don't count on it!

David decides to do a head count in chapter 21.
It seems like a good idea — after all, God asked
Moses to number the people back in, erm, Numbers.
But this time there's a problem.

👁 Read 1 Chronicles 21 v 1–8

ENGAGE YOUR BRAIN

- ▶ Who is behind David's idea? (v1)
- ▶ What was Joab's response? (v3)
- ▶ And God's? (v7)
- ▶ What do you think David might have been starting to rely on?
- ▶ What does David recognise? (v8)

Satan might have put the idea in David's head, but it was David's decision to go ahead despite Joab's opposition. Maybe he was starting to take pride in his mighty army instead of remembering that it was God who gave him the victory.

👁 Read verses 9–30

- ▶ What choice does God give David? (v9–12)
- ▶ What does David choose? Why?
- ▶ What would you choose?
- ▶ How fierce was God's judgment? (v14–16)
- ▶ How great is His mercy? (v27)
- ▶ How was the threat of God's judgment removed? (v26–27)
- ▶ So what does David decide? (22 v 1)

Human sin. God's judgment. Sacrifice. God's mercy. The same old pattern. Even the spot for the temple is chosen on that basis; a place where God's judgment is averted by sacrifice. David's sin brought Jerusalem to the brink of destruction. Now the temple — the focus for forgiveness from God's judgment — would be built on the spot where God rescued His people.

PRAY ABOUT IT

Our sin deserves God's punishment. But Jesus paid the ultimate sacrifice so that you could be shown mercy. Talk to Him about that now.

THE BOTTOM LINE

Sin. Judgment. Sacrifice. Mercy.

→ TAKE IT FURTHER

Grab more on page 124.

85 | Be prepared

David wanted to build a temple for God in Jerusalem.
But God said: "No, your son, Solomon, will build it."
But David was so excited about the temple he started
making lavish preparations for the building work.

👁 **Read 1 Chronicles 22 v 1–10**

ENGAGE YOUR BRAIN

▶ David has got his heart set on getting the temple built — who does he start by organising? (v2–4)

▶ Then who does his attention turn to? (v5–6)

▶ Why wasn't David allowed to build the temple? (v8)

▶ What was the news for Solomon? (v9–10)

👁 **Read verses 11–16**

▶ What does David pray for Solomon?

▶ What does he remind him?

▶ How does he encourage him?

👁 **Read verses 17–19**

▶ Who does David start to organise next? (v17)

▶ What does he want their priority to be? (v19)

▶ How will they show that?

Read verses 6–19 again. Spot any words that are repeated a lot?

David is concerned for the honour of God's name. He wants Solomon and all the people to share that passion. It's his greatest desire as he faces his own death (v5).

PRAY ABOUT IT

The first line of the Lord's Prayer says: "Our Father in Heaven, hallowed be your name". It's a prayer for God's name — His character and reputation — to be honoured. Why not make that your prayer today?

THE BOTTOM LINE

Devote your heart and soul to seeking the Lord your God.

➡ **TAKE IT FURTHER**

Be prepared for more on page 125.

86 | Listed building

David's really got his mind on the job. He's making sure Solomon has all the resources — physical and human — to build God's new temple.

Skim read 1 Chronicles 23–26

ENGAGE YOUR BRAIN

▶ There's a LOT of information here. So skim these chapters and list below what sort of jobs are needed:

▶ What tribe do they all come from? (Did you spot it?)

▶ Why is this important?

God provided everything David and Solomon would need, and He provided the people to build and minister in the temple. The Levites were set apart for this special task, but remember ALL Christians are now priests in God's service. Wow.

GET ON WITH IT

Being part of God's people means getting involved! We are not spectators at a show but participants in a family. Are you serving, praying for and meeting with God's family? If not, why not?

PRAY ABOUT IT

Ask God to show you how you can best serve Him as a part of His family.

THE BOTTOM LINE

God has a job for you to do.

→ TAKE IT FURTHER

Get to work on page 125.

87 Divide and conquer

Don't mention the census (ooops, just did!) but
here's an overview of Israel's fighting capabilities
as David hands over to Solomon.

👁 Read 1 Chronicles 27 v 1–24

ENGAGE YOUR BRAIN

▷ When were each division on
duty? (v1)

▷ Good way of organising things?

▷ Anyone famous among the
officers? (v18)

▷ Why did David stop short of
numbering those below fighting
age? (v23)

▷ What are we reminded of in v24?

👁 Read verses 25–34

▷ Who are named in verses 25–34?

▷ What were their responsibilities?

David is leaving everything in good
shape for Solomon. But this is all a
bit of a sad reminder that human
kings don't go on for ever. David was
a great king but he died. He was not
God's promised, perfect King.

PRAY ABOUT IT

Thank God for Jesus, our forever
King.

THE BOTTOM LINE

Jesus' throne endures for ever.

→ TAKE IT FURTHER

Find the forever King on page 125.

88 | Loyal royal

Famous last words. Sometimes they're short: "Either that wallpaper goes or I do". David's are a bit longer (and much more serious).

👁 Read 1 Chronicles 28 v 1–10

▷ Who does David address one of his last big speeches to? (v1)

▷ What does he call them? (v2)

▷ What does he remind them of? (v4–7)

▷ What does he command them? (v8)

▷ What does he expect of Solomon? (v9–10)

-
-
-
-

God has made awesome promises to David and his family AND He has kept them. David warns the people not to turn their backs on such an awesome and faithful God.

👁 Read verses 11–21

▷ What preparations has David made? (v11)

▷ Where did all these plans come from? (v12, 19)

▷ How does David encourage Solomon? (v20–21)

👁 Read 1 Chronicles 29 v 1–9

▷ How does David keep Solomon humble? (v1)

▷ How do the people respond to all David's words? (v6–9)

▷ And David's reaction? (v9)

PRAY ABOUT IT

God is faithful: we are not. Thank Him now that Jesus dealt with our faithlessness at the cross and can change our hearts by His Holy Spirit. Ask Him to keep you trusting in Jesus today and always.

THE BOTTOM LINE

God is faithful.

→ TAKE IT FURTHER

Shortest *Take it further* ever – p125.

89 | Back to the future

"And now, the end is near, and so I face the final curtain" — that's the case now for David and for the book of 1 Chronicles!

👁 **Read 1 Chronicles 29 v 10–20**

▷ Who do David's thoughts and words turn to at the end? (v10)

▷ What does he praise God for? (v10–13)

▷ What does David still find hard to understand? (v14)

▷ What does he recognise about humans? (v15)

▷ What does he ask God for? (v18–19)

▷ How do the people respond? (v20)

👁 **Read verses 21–30**

▷ How do they go about crowning Solomon? (v21–22)

▷ How was life under King Sol? (v23–24)

▷ How does God bless Solomon? (v25)

▷ Are David's prayers answered?

David might die "at a good old age, having enjoyed long life, wealth and honour", and that may be the best way to go, but he still went. Death was unavoidable. But David knew the Lord and he had a glimpse of what was to come — the defeat of death and eternal life with the Lord.

PRAY ABOUT IT

Thank God that, as Christians, we can see clearly because God's grace has now "been revealed through the appearing of our Saviour, Christ Jesus, who has destroyed death and has brought life and immortality to light through the gospel" (2 Timothy 1 v 10).

THE BOTTOM LINE

Walk God's way in this life... but death is not the end!

→ **TAKE IT FURTHER**

Bye bye 1 Chronicles! Page 125.

90 | Times of trouble

We've read about King David's military successes. But it wasn't always easy for him. Many times he was surrounded by vicious enemies, wondering if he'd survive. He wrote this psalm in one of those moments.

Read Psalm 141

ENGAGE YOUR BRAIN

▶ Where does David turn in his hour of need? (v1)

▶ What is he most concerned about at the start of this psalm? (v3–4)

Incredible. In the face of great provoking, he asks God for self-control, not to retaliate with vicious words (v3) or get involved in his opponents' dirty tactics (v4). But only to be remembered for speaking with gracious words (v6). And he's even ready to face fair criticism (v5).

▶ What has this time of trouble made him realise? (v8)

▶ What does this tell us about David's trust?

▶ How will this help you in times of trouble?

THINK IT OVER

▶ Is there anything you need rescuing from?

▶ What evil are you drawn towards?

▶ What do you need to ask God?

▶ And what can you praise Him for?

PRAY ABOUT IT

Now write your own version of this psalm, reflecting your situation, your sin, your needs, your experience of God's goodness.

Then read it (or sing it) to God.

→ TAKE IT FURTHER

Tough it out on page 125.

91 Dave in a cave

David wrote this psalm before he became king. He was on the run from murderous King Saul, hiding in a cave.

👁 Read Psalm 142

ENGAGE YOUR BRAIN

▶ *How was David feeling? (v1)*

▶ *So what did he do? (v2)*

▶ *How is this an example to you when times are tough?*

▶ *How do you tend to react?*

▶ *What else do we learn about David's situation? (v3–4)*

▶ *What did he tell God? (v5)*

David had been abandoned and opposed by so many people, but God had not abandoned him. He knew God was his "refuge" (a place to escape to for safety) and his "portion" (satisfaction).

▶ *Did David bottle up his emotions? (v6)*

▶ *What did he admit about himself?*

Tough times are opportunities to trust God.

▶ *Is that how you see them?*

▶ *How does this psalm give you confidence?*

PRAY ABOUT IT

It also encourages us to tell God how we feel. To admit it to Him when things get on top of us. To ask Him for help. So ask.

→ TAKE IT FURTHER

Final word on page 125.

TAKE IT FURTHER

If you want a little more at the end of each day's study, this is where you come. The TAKE IT FURTHER sections give you something extra. They look at some of the issues covered in the day's study, pose deeper questions, and point you to the big picture of the whole Bible.

MARK

Jesus: A marked man

1 – WHITER THAN WHITE
Read Luke 9 v 28–36 for Luke's version of events.

▷ *What extra info do we get here? (v30–31)*

They were talking about Jesus' death. Peter had realised that Jesus was the Christ (Mark 8 v 29) but he and the others hadn't fully understood who Jesus was and why He came. Even when they saw His glory. They hadn't grasped that Jesus was far greater than Moses or Elijah. The voice of God spelled it out to them: "This is my Son... listen to Him." Listen to Jesus first, above anyone or anything else.

Listening to Jesus means taking the Bible seriously. Grab a notebook or create a file on your PC. Divide it up into sections called *"Bible passage"*, *"What it teaches about Jesus"*, *"What I've learned"* and *"What I'm going to do about it"*. Every time you read about Jesus in the Bible, fill it in.

2 – FAITH THE TRUTH
Maybe in the past God has worked through you to encourage another Christian or to answer someone's prayer. Great! But is there a danger you'll assume this automatically means you'll do the same again?

▷ *How will you remember to keep relying on God?*

3 – FIRST THINGS LAST
Read Matthew 18 v 1–6

▷ *What else did Jesus say about children?*
v3:
v4:
v5:
v6:

Children were unimportant in that society: to be looked after, but not to be looked up to. Jesus' action (v2) was shocking; His teaching (v3–5) was even more so. Disciples should be willing to be like children — insignificant, unimpressive, willing to be nobodies. Such a change isn't just for those who already follow Jesus. It's the only way to become a Christian — realising you're nothing without Jesus.

4 – TEAM MATES
Check out Philippians 2 v 2–11
- ▶ How should people united to Christ treat each other? (v2)
- ▶ What's the key to unity? (v3–4)
- ▶ How is Jesus the ultimate example of v3–4?
- ▶ How far did Jesus go in serving others? (v8)
- ▶ Where is Jesus now? (v9)
- ▶ How does that encourage Christians who are suffering for Christ?

5 – CUT IT OUT
Read verses 43–48 again and then Isaiah 66 v 22–24
Hell, as Jesus teaches, is awful. Severe injury is a much better prospect. Hell is unending punishment and it's part of God's promises. Taking hell seriously means taking your sin seriously. Do you do that?

6 – THE D-WORD
- ▶ What makes Jesus' teaching on divorce unpopular today?
- ▶ Will you trust that God's way is best?
- ▶ What reasons will you use to defend it?
- ▶ In what situations do you need to remind yourself that God's way is always best?

7 – CHILDISH BEHAVIOUR
Jesus' views on marriage and divorce were controversial (see study 6). And so was what He said about children. Kids were seen and not heard, and were definitely looked down on. So the disciples trying to get rid of the kids hanging around Jesus was just what people did back then. But Jesus didn't like that attitude. Children matter, and have much to teach us. Their trust, simplicity and dependence are all things Christians should show in their relationship with God and with other believers.

8 – MONEY TALKS
- ▶ What kind of things do people say you need to have a good life?
- ▶ What kind of things is it easy to think you need to do to deserve eternal life?

Remember, all you need to do is trust in Jesus. Nothing else! Being good and being rich doesn't bring full life, now or in eternity — only following Jesus does.

9 – FAME AND FORTUNE
Read verse 45 again
A ransom was paid to set a prisoner or slave free.
- ▶ How will you use v45 when people say Jesus' death was just a great shame, or a heroic but pointless act?

It's easy to badmouth the disciples for being stupid here.
- ▶ But how do we fall into the same trap of seeking recognition and reputation — perhaps in more subtle ways?

NEHEMIAH
Big build-up

11 – CITY IN RUINS

Read Nehemiah 1 v 1–3 again

Three key words occur here:

a) **Remnant:** Those who survived the exile. God would keep His promises through them (Isaiah 10 v 20–22).

b) **Jerusalem:** God's city, which He promised to restore (Isaiah 60 v 10–15).

c) **Disgrace:** A sign of God's judgment, which He'd promised to remove (Ezekiel 36 v 15, 30).

In chapters 1–3, Nehemiah's big concerns are a) the people, and b) the city. The book charts the progress of them both. For the city it's up-up-up; for the people it's up-down-up-down. Increasingly, throughout the book, the question is whether the people have *reformed* while the city is being *rebuilt*. Nehemiah wanted to see God honoured among His people again. Would that happen?

12 – NERVOUS QUESTIONS

▶ *How do prayer and action work together for Nehemiah?*

▶ *Can you think about a time when prayer and actions worked together in the life of Jesus? (Hint: Matthew 26 v 39–46)*

▶ *How can they work together for you?*

13 – HOPE IN RUINS

One writer has summed up the punch line of the whole Bible as "the Lamb". However depressing things around us may look, we know that Jesus has already defeated all His enemies decisively and one day the whole world will see that. Encourage yourself by reading **Philippians 2 v 5–11** and **Revelation 22 v 1–5**.

14 – GATE EXPECTATIONS

Read Ephesians 4 v 11–16

▶ *How do God's people in the New Testament work together for a common purpose?*

▶ *What is being built up here? (v12)*

▶ *Is everyone's contribution identical? (v11)*

▶ *What is the aim of the church? (v15–16)*

15 – PRAYER IN ACTION

Mockery and persecution are unfortunately part of the Christian life (see what Jesus faced for doing God's will in Matthew 27 v 41–44).

▶ *But what is the encouragement for us in Matthew 5 v 10–12?*

16 – PREPARED FOR BATTLE

Look back through chapter 4. Which parts show Nehemiah's...

a) common sense?

b) trust in God?

c) flexibility?

d) own example to others?

e) awareness of history?

17 – TROUBLE WITHIN

See how the apostle Paul has the same attitude as Nehemiah in **I Corinthians 9 v 1–23**.

- ▶ *What rights could Paul have claimed? (v4–5)*
- ▶ *What point does Paul make in v7–10?*
- ▶ *Yet had Paul taken payment for his gospel work? (v12)*
- ▶ *What responsibility do we have for Christians who spread the gospel? (v13–14)*
- ▶ *Why didn't Paul boast about his work or take payment? (v16–18)*
- ▶ *Why did Paul give up a lot of his rights and privileges? (v19)*
- ▶ *What did Paul do to spread the message that Jesus saves? (v20–22)*
- ▶ *Why? (v23)*

Jesus sacrificed His life to rescue sinners like us. Paul was telling people about Jesus and made sacrifices too. He wasn't in it for the money or fame — his reward was the joy of sharing the gospel with anyone and everyone. The message of Jesus is free for all. And it's a privilege to tell people about Jesus, not a chore.

18 – FIGHTING TALK

What intimidates you and stops you living whole heartedly for Jesus? Perhaps it's worrying what people will say or think about you. Or maybe you'll run into conflict with your family. Why do you think these things have such a negative impact on you? What does God say about

them? Can you think of a Bible verse that might help? Ask God to strengthen you.

19 – FINISHED!

- ▶ *Do you think a Christian dating someone who isn't a Christian is the same kind of issue we see here with Tobiah being married to a Jewish girl?*
- ▶ *Why / why not?*

Check out the following Bible verses and be honest with yourself about the problems which might arise.
**Read Nehemiah 13 v 26,
then 1 Corinthians 7 v 39
and 2 Corinthians 6 v 14-18.**

Is there any way that you are currently "yoked with unbelievers"? Paul doesn't mean that we should have nothing to do with non-Christians, or how would we ever get to share the gospel with them? He's talking about close relationships (like cattle "yoked" together to plough fields!) where we are likely to be contaminated by ungodly ideas and dragged away from Jesus. This is one major reason why it's a bad idea to start dating someone who doesn't believe in Jesus.

20 – LISTED BUILDING

Read Revelation 21 v 1–4, 10–27 and 22 v 1–5

- ▶ *What will life in the New Jerusalem be like?*

The Bible doesn't actually tell us much about eternal life. But what it does tell us is tantalising. Most importantly, God will live with His people — in fact He'll bring heaven down to us! Heaven and earth will be united: the original relationship between God and humans, which existed in the Garden of Eden, will be restored. There will be no more sadness or suffering.

PROVERBS

21 – LIVING FOR GOD

▷ *What are we told about foolishness?*
  v7:
  v16:
  v21:
  v24:
  v28:

▷ *How does a wise person live?*
  v9:
  v10:
  v14:
  v17:
  v24:
  v27:

22 – HEARING AID

Read Proverbs 18 v 10–11
▷ *Where do you look for security?*

Read Luke 12 v 13–21
▷ *What is the man in Jesus' story most worried about? (v16–18)*
▷ *What's he looking forward to? (v19)*
▷ *What does God think of him? And why? (v20–21)*
▷ *What point is Jesus making? (end of v15)*

Both the man talking to Jesus and the guy in the parable focus on storing up things for themselves for this life.

▷ *What should their priority be (v21)?*

23 – WISE WORDS FROM GOD

Read verse 17, then Matthew 25 v 34–40
If you're a Christian, you're a subject of King Jesus — and look how much He loves you! You're so close to Him that He sees something kind done for you as being done for Him; if something nasty is done to you, He sees it as nastiness towards Him. And one day, He'll give you everything that's His (v34). That's how much He cares about you! Of course He also expects you to show love for Him by being kind to other believers.

▷ *Think of one specific way you can do that today/tomorrow.*

24 – JUST THE ONE

Does your chosen verse have any parallels elsewhere in the Bible? Try to find a concordance or cross-reference Bible. Or ask someone you know who knows their Bible well.

For example, for v1, see Prov 23 v 29–35.
For v4, see Prov 6 v 6–11.
For v9, see 1 John 1 v 8.

▷ *What do the parallel verses add to your understanding?*

MARK

26 – A MARKED MAN

Read Zechariah 9 v 9–17

▶ *Why the huge joy? (v9)*

▶ *What would their King be like and what would He do? (v9–10)*

God promised to send a perfect King to rescue His people. But Jesus wouldn't be the usual warrior king — His reign would bring peace, righteousness and rescue.

God will restore His people and then use them to defeat His enemies. The message of Jesus is peace with God for those who trust in Him, but destruction for those who fight against Him. We need to remember both sides of the gospel. And as you struggle to tell people the truth, you can take comfort from verses 15–17. God will protect you and one day you'll sparkle like a jewel in a crown for Him!

27 – TURNING THE TABLES

Read verse 15 again

The temple seemed to be thriving, busy with people coming to offer sacrifices. So what was Jesus' problem?

a) **No reality.** No spiritual life, just empty religion. It was no longer a place for prayer, but for fruitless ritual and money-making.

▶ *It's great to go to church / youth group regularly, but what trap might we fall into?*

▶ *How will you combat this danger?*

b) **No recognition.** Although the whole Old Testament was focused on the coming of the Christ, the temple-goers missed Him when He turned up in the flesh. Fatal. Ask God to help you alert your friends to Jesus' warning about those who fail to recognise Him for who He really is.

28 – FIGS AND FAITH

For a masterclass on prayer by Jesus, flick to **Matthew 6 v 5–15**.

30 – HORROR STORY

Read Isaiah 5 v 1–7

God's done all the work, but the vineyard — His ungrateful people — produces only bad fruit. But God doesn't destroy it: He gives it to others. (Also see Psalm 80 v 8–19). Israel had pride of place of place as God's people. But when they reject Jesus and show they're not truly His, God turns to those who do acknowledge His Son as King — whether they're Jews or non–Jews.

31 – TAXING QUESTION

Look at verses 16–17

The Roman denarius coin had an image of Emperor Tiberius Caesar on one side. On the other side it said: "Tiberius Caesar Augustus, son of the divine Augustus". It was claiming Emperor Caesar was a god and should be worshipped. In distinguishing clearly between Caesar and God, Jesus was cleverly attacking the idolatrous claims made on the coins.

32 – WIFE AFTER DEATH

Read 1 Corinthians 15 v 35–58

God overcomes death every time a seed sprouts to life (v37–38). So raising the dead is easy for God. Everything God has created has been given the right body for its situation (v38–41). And when Christians are raised to live with God for ever, they'll be given new, perfect bodies (v42–44). We've been made in Adam's likeness but when we're raised to eternal life we'll be made like Jesus ("the last Adam") with new spiritual bodies.

▷ *What can Christians expect to happen? (v51–52)*

▷ *Why don't we need to fear death?*

▷ *If all this is true, how should Christians live? (v58)*

Only God knows when all this will happen. But we have His promise that it will, and that we'll be more like Jesus. Until that day, life can be a hassle, but we know we're on the winning side over death and our own sin (v57). Jesus has already won victory for Christians, so they should live lives that show this — standing firm and giving their all to serve Jesus.

33 – GREAT QUESTION!

Read Deuteronomy 6 v 1–5

"The Lord is one" (v4) — God is the only true God and should be the only one His people worship, love and obey. That's why God's people must love the Lord completely, with their whole lives (v5). They must treat His words seriously,

teaching them to kids and talking about them all the time.

34 – SON OF DAVID

Read Psalm 110

▷ *What will God do for the person David's singing about?*

v1:

v2:

v3:

This psalm is really about Jesus. About His return to God's presence after being raised from the dead. On the cross, Jesus defeated all His enemies — and will finally dispose of them on the day He returns as Judge. Use this psalm to help you thank God for Jesus — for what He has done and what He will do.

35 – FAKE OR FAITHFUL?

Read 2 Corinthians 8 v 6–15

▷ *What was the Corinthian attitude towards giving? (v10)*

▷ *How does Paul encourage them? (v6–8, 11–12)*

▷ *How should Christian generosity work? (13–15)*

Marxism is famous for the saying: "From each according to his ability, to each according to his need". But that's actually a Bible principle!

▷ *Who is the greatest giver of all (v9)?*

▷ *How rich was Jesus?*

▷ *How poor did He become?*

▷ *How rich are we?*

Do you need to review how you give your time, talents and money? Make definite plans and then stick to them.

37 – LASTING LOVE
Read Genesis chapter 1
Pause every few verses to praise and thank God.

NEHEMIAH

38 – BIG BUILD-UP
Do you know what it means to really rejoice in the Lord? Even if our circumstances are tough (like Paul's were when he wrote to the Philippians from prison) we can rejoice in God's goodness in all that He has done for us. And all that He has secured for us in the future.

Read Philippians 4 v 4–7
▶ Why not learn it by heart?

39 – BRANCHING OUT
When you read the Bible, do you ask God to help you to understand it and obey it by the power of His Spirit? It's very easy to rest on our own abilities but we'll miss the point and remain the same. If you haven't already – pray that prayer and then look at the whole thing again. **Psalm 119 v 18** is a great prayer to use.

40 – HISTORY LESSON
Read verses 1–6 again
Those are two things we should do when we pray:
1. Confess. We should talk to God about

the wrong things we've done and say sorry to Him.
2. Worship. We should praise God for the great things He has done.

The Israelites looked back on their history to see how great God had been to them in the past. Try writing a brief history of your life, showing how God has been good to you over the years. Then use it regularly to help you thank God in your prayers.

41 – GOD IS GREAT!
Read Acts chapter 7
▶ Notice any similarities to Nehemiah chapter 9?
▶ What does Stephen add that is worse than all the previous sins committed by God's people?
▶ How does God amazingly use that crime to show His justice, compassion and faithfulness?

42 – PROMISING FUTURE
Read Matthew 22 v 36–40
▶ How does Jesus sum up the Old Testament Law?
▶ Can we possibly keep that command?
▶ Did Jesus?
▶ How does 2 Corinthians 5 v 21 give us confidence?

43 – ON THE MOVE
Remind yourself of God's foundational promises to His people given to Abraham (Abram) in **Genesis 12 v 1–3**.
▶ How are these all fulfilled in Jesus?

115

44 – CELEBRATION NATION

Look again at the description of the New Jerusalem in **Revelation 21 v 1 – 22 v 5**. How is it better than the Jerusalem of Nehemiah's day? Make a list.

-
-
-
-
-
-
-
-
-
-
-

45 – PRAISE PARTY

God is praised now and for ever. Read these verses and u se them to help you praise Him:
Exodus 15 v 1–18
Psalm 103
Revelation 7 v 9–12

46 – TIME TO CHANGE

Praising and worshipping God isn't just about singing or praying. Take a look at **John 14 v 15** and **Romans 12 v 1–2**.

▷ *Does that challenge you?*
▷ *In what areas?*

Talk to God about them.

47 – TROUBLE IN STORE

It's easy to be intimidated by other people — scared they will mock you or even harm you for standing out as a Christian. But read what **Matthew 10 v 28** says. Why not learn **Proverbs 29 v 25** off by heart and then pray for the strength to live that way.

48 – TROUBLE AND STRIFE

The last chapter of Nehemiah is a bit of a damp squib. The construction work has been completed but the people's hearts are as unreconstructed as ever. What do the people need? Read **Jeremiah 31 v 31–34** and **Ezekiel 36 v 25–27** — they and we need a Messiah! Thank God for Jesus, who gives us a much needed heart transplant!

Situation at the end of Nehemiah

Old Testament prophets foretold the fall and rise of God's exiled people. With a new temple in a new creation. And a great King. But Nehemiah ends in anti-climax...

- The glory of the temple never equalled that of Solomon's.
- The city was a poor copy of what it once was.
- The people were now just a "remnant" under the rule of pagan kings.
- There was no great king from David's line.
- The people were still rebelling against God. They were home but nothing had really improved.

The story of Nehemiah ends with a tension

between the promises of God (Genesis 12 v 1–3; Ezekiel 40–48; Isaiah 40–66) and the experience of the people, who were rejecting God and so not enjoying a perfect life with Him. Conclusion: there must be more! Which leaves us waiting... for Jesus.

Jesus fulfilled the Old Testament prophecies

1. Jesus broke the power of sin (Romans 8 v 3–4).
2. He brought to an end all Old Testament rituals, establishing permanent forgiveness and better access to God (Hebrews 7–10).
3. He is the promised King from David's line, and will rule for ever .
4. Believers will one day live in perfect rest with Jesus (Hebrews 4).
5. There will be a new, eternal Jerusalem (Revelation 21 v 1–4).

49 – BY THE RIVERS OF BABYLON
In Revelation, Babylon stands for godless society — people who reject God.
Read Revelation 18 v 1–8

▶ *How is Babylon described? (v2–3)*
▶ *Why must God's people keep away from Babylon? (v4)*
▶ *What will happen to Babylon? (v8)*

There are so many temptations in the world — sex and wealth (v3) are two of the biggest ones. It's easy to think that, as Christians, we're immune to these temptations, without noticing they're

already seducing us.

Read Revelation 19 v 1–5

▶ *Why is life with God better than life without Him? (v1–2)*
▶ *What's the response once God's enemies have been defeated? (v5)*

It's not popular to talk about God's judgment. But we must remember that any punishment from God is totally fair. In fact, God's judgment is a cause for celebration. We can praise and thank God for being true and fair and punishing evil as well as rescuing His people.

51 – SAFE WITH GOD
If God knows everything about me, aren't I just a robot with no free will?

Read 1 Peter 2 v 9–12

▶ *Why has God chosen us? (v9)*
▶ *Did we deserve the rescue God brought? (v10)*

In His mercy, God has chosen people, so that they'll praise Him — and that's a response that can only come from the heart. God's in control, yet He wants us to give Him the honour He deserves.

▶ *Will you complain about His power or praise Him for His mercy?*

1 CHRONICLES
Walk this way

52 – ROYAL RECORD

1 and 2 Chronicles are actually one book that has been split in two.

1 Chron 1–9: Family trees
1 Chron 10 – 2 Chron 9: The kingdom under David and Solomon, faithfully serving God
2 Chron 10–36: Judah ruled (mostly) by godless wasters

What's the difference between Chronicles and the Samuel and Kings books?
a) Chronicles has all those genealogies (family trees).
b) It only gives Saul one chapter.
c) It says little about David's and Solomon's personal failings.
d) It concentrates on the kings of Judah (the smaller southern kingdom), not Israel (the bigger northern kingdom).
e) It's the only one to mention the return from exile.

53 – PRAYER OF PAIN

Read Hebrews 12 v 1–13 and think about how you would use it to answer someone who says we can pray the prayer of Jabez and expect to see it answered today.

▶ *What will our day-to-day Christian life be like?*
▶ *Why is this? (v7)*

▶ *What should be the result of this? (v10–11)*

God uses tough times in life both to discipline us and help us keep going. Only parents who don't love their children don't discipline them and encourage them in the right way of living. Life as a Christian may be painful at times, but God is constantly training us and making us more like Him.

54 – ENTERING THE PROMISED LAND

Some people take issue with God getting rid of the land's original inhabitants (v40, 43), saying it's like genocide or ethnic cleansing.

Read the commands in **Deuteronomy 7 v 2; 20 v 17** (The accounts of this [not fully] happening are in Joshua 6–7, 11 and 1 Samuel 1).

BUT: Make sure you read these commands carefully in context. What reasons does God give for such severe measures?
Deuteronomy 7 v 1–26
Deuteronomy 9 v 4
Deuteronomy 12 v 31
Deuteronomy 20 v 16–18
Also: Exodus 34 v 11–16
and Hebrews 11 v 31

55 – THE BEST INHERITANCE

If you think back to those promises God made to Abraham, David and co, remember that they are all fulfilled in Jesus. What about the land one? Well, one day Christians will inherit new heavens and a new earth (2 Peter 3 v 13). But even now we have arrived — we are already IN Christ. It's pretty mind-boggling but an amazing truth!

See John 17 v 20–25
Romans 8 v 1
Ephesians 1 v 13
Colossians 3 v 3

56 – FAMILY PLANNING

Bible family trees don't do much for you? Well, think what they show about God's purposes and promises. Think how it could have helped the first readers of Chronicles to rediscover their roots in David's line.

▷ *What would all this have taught them about God?*
▷ *What hope could it have given them?*
▷ *What challenge did it raise for them, do you think?*

Today we live after the arrival of Jesus, born into David's line. The Bible says those who trust Jesus are God's people now.

▷ *So how should we be encouraged by looking back?*
▷ *What's the way to enjoy all He's promised us?*

57 – SAUL STRIKES OUT

Jesus tells His disciples: "You are my friends if you do what I command" (John 15 v 14). It's impossible to keep God's commands in our own strength, but Jesus gives us His Holy Spirit to enable us to walk His way. Ask for His help now to put **James 1 v 22–25** into practice when you read the Bible.

58 – DAVID STEPS FORWARD

To really get the significance of God's king being a shepherd, compare God's promise to David in v2 with **Ezekiel 34** and **John 10 v 11–18**. Wow. Talk to God about what you've learned.

59 – MIGHTY MEN

▷ *Which of these "mighty men" most stands out to you?*
▷ *Why?*

These men did incredibly brave feats, but not to make themselves look great. They were in the service of God and His king, David. They didn't seem to boast of their strength and courage. It was given to them by God so they used it to please Him.

▷ *What abilities and passions has God given you?*
▷ *How can you use them to serve Him?*
▷ *How can you use them to help/serve Christian leaders?*
▷ *So what exactly are you going to do?*

Ask God to give you the strength, courage and ability to serve Him. Pray for His help to do the things you've decided to do.

60 – JOIN IN!

When the Christian politician and campaigner William Wilberforce began his campaign to outlaw the slave trade, he faced colossal opposition. Slowly but surely, over a period of many years, God brought down his opponents and changed public opinion. Why not read more

119

about his life — there are plenty of good Christian biographies like *The Freedom Fighter* by Derick Bingham or *Amazing Grace in the Life of William Wilberforce* by John Piper.

61 – ARK AND RIDE

In the popular Narnia books, the children are constantly reminded that Aslan (the Jesus figure) is "not a tame lion". On being asked if he is "safe", Mr Beaver replies: "Who said anything about safe? 'Course he isn't safe. But he's good. He's the King, I tell you."

Our God is not tame — He is holy, awesome and terrifying, but like Aslan, He is good. **Read Revelation 1 v 12–18.**

2 & 3 JOHN

Sure signs

62 – TRUTH AND LOVE

Read verses 1–2 again
Then read 1 John 3 v 24 and 4 v 15
John speaks about the truth dwelling in us — and also about God's Spirit dwelling in us.

▶ *Why do these two go together?*
▶ *What lessons are there for us from this?*

Christians have such a close relationship with God that His Spirit lives in them, helping them to love Him, to live for Him and to love others.

63 – LOVE LIFE

Read 1 John 2 v 3–6

▶ *What's a big sign that we know Jesus personally? (v3, 6)*
▶ *How did Jesus "walk"?*

God's love is made complete in Christians — they truly love God. And they show this by obeying Him, walking His way (v5–6). OK, we can't hope to live perfect lives as Jesus did. But we can live more and more for Him, changing, becoming more like Jesus, giving our lives to Him.

64 – WATCH OUT!

Read verses 10–11 again

▶ *When members of a cult or sect knock on your door, how do you handle it?*
▶ *What should Christians do in view of 2 John?*
▶ *How can we be prepared for when they come calling?*

Well, in advance we can...
1) Pray; 2) Think: "Do I know my Bible well enough to handle a conversation?"; 3) Read about what that particular sect believes; 4) Remember it's possible (and maybe wise) to refuse in a loving way; 5) Ask an older Christian to be there too, to explain the Bible clearly and point them to Christ; 6) get prepared for the next time.

66 – SERVING SUGGESTION

▶ *What do these verses teach you about hospitality?*

Romans 12 v 13–16
Hebrews 13 v 1–2
1 Peter 4 v 8–11

▶ *Why should we be so welcoming? (Matthew 10 v 40–42)?*
▶ *How exactly will you be more welcoming?*

67 – SPOT THE DIFFERENCE

Look back at the box in study 66.
▶ *What did you say you'd do?*
▶ *How's it going?*
▶ *If you've not done anything yet, what will you do about it?*
▶ *What do you need to pray?*

PROVERBS

68 – LIVING FOR GOD

Read chapter 21 again, thinking about our plans and God's plans.
▶ *How do you see human planning and God's over-ruling in this chapter?*
▶ *How should this make you pray?*
▶ *And plan?*

Look at verses 2, 4 and 21
Proverbs always asks us to dig below the surface, exposing our hearts — what we're really like.
▶ *How lightly or seriously do you take what God says?*

69 – RICH AND POOR

▶ **Read Deuteronomy 15 v 7–11**
▶ *How were God's people to treat those with less money? (v7–8)*
▶ *What attitude should they have? (v10)*
▶ *How would God bless them? (v10)*

For Christians, Jesus has cancelled the biggest debt of all — sin. Because of our sin, we owe God our lives. We deserve to be punished with eternal death, but Jesus took the cost Himself. He was punished and died in our place. He cancelled our debt. Our sins were wiped out. Forgiven.

▶ *Any Christians you know who are struggling to make ends meet?*
▶ *Who can you help out?*
▶ *How will you do it?*

70 – WISE UP

Read verses 24–25 again
And then Proverbs 1 v 10–19
▶ *How do you behave when you're around your friends?*
▶ *Do you go along with the crowd or obey God?*
▶ *Who encourages you to do stuff you know is wrong?*
▶ *What should you do about it?*
▶ *How will you avoid temptation?*

71 – CENTRAL DEFENDER

Read Psalm 46
It sounds as though the world is falling apart. Yet this guy knows that God never leaves His people and always defends them and helps them through

troubled times.

ⓘ *Why is God's city safe? (v5)*

ⓘ *What happens to God's enemies? (v6)*

ⓘ *How would you describe God's power? (v8–9)*

ⓘ *How should we respond to this terrifying God? (v10)*

The Bible shows us over and over how immensely powerful the Lord is. Yet He wants us to know Him (v10) and have a close relationship with Him. Jesus has made this possible. And God protects His people, who will one day live with Him in His city.

72 – DRUNK AND DISORDERLY

Read Proverbs 20 v 1, 1 Corinthians 6 v 19–20, Ephesians 5 v 18, and James 5 v 16.

If you're tempted by heavy drinking, talk to another Christian about it, so they can pray for you and check up on you.

73 – WORDS OF WISDOM

Read verse 11 again and then Isaiah 58 v 6–12

ⓘ *What did God want from His people? (v6–7)*

ⓘ *What will happen if God's people live like this?*

v8:

v9:

v11:

v12:

ⓘ *How can you fight injustice?*

ⓘ *Who's worse off than you who you could share stuff with?*

74 – FAIR ENOUGH

Read verse 29 again followed by Romans 12 v 17–21

ⓘ *What's the command here? (v17)*

ⓘ *Why? (v19)*

ⓘ *What should we do when we're treated badly? (v20–21)*

ⓘ *Who gives you a hard time?*

ⓘ *So how can you make peace with them and treat them lovingly?*

ⓘ *Anything you need to stop doing?*

75 – DESPERATE SITUATION

Read James 3 v 2–6

Is anyone perfect in what they say? (v2)

What is the tongue compared to?

What huge effect can our words have on our lives? (v5–6)

If we manage to mostly control our tongues, it shows we have great self-control. But the person who lets their tongue run away with them is in danger of destruction (v6). If we don't control what we say, it can completely corrupt us.

ⓘ *In what specific ways has your tongue taken over this week?*

ⓘ *Who have you offended or said nasty things about?*

ⓘ *What do you need to do about it?*

Talk to God about these issues right now.

1 CHRONICLES

76 – WALK THIS WAY

The Old Testament is full of predictions that one day all the nations will flock to God's city — see **Psalm 86 v 9** for example. What we see starting to happen here with David (and even more so with Solomon) will find its ultimate fulfilment in **Revelation 21 v 22–27**. Take some time to read it and think about that reality now.

77 – ARK LIFE

Read Matthew 5 v 11–12

Why not try and learn it so you can remember what Jesus says the next time people give you a hard time for being a Christian?

78 –THANKS, GOD!

You used to have to be a Levite to get close to God and serve Him. Not any more. Why?
Look at Revelation 1 v 4–6 and 5 v 6–10

79 – LASTING LOVE

David wanted the world to recognise God as He really is. And for people to honour God, from the heart, for what He'd done.

Maybe your life isn't tons of fun right now. But it's always right that we thank God for the cross and for the times we've seen God be good to us. Will you thank Him right now?

80 – HOUSE PARTY

Look at verses 10–14 again

There's a bit of a play on words with the idea of "house" here. It can mean a literal house or a dynasty. Notice how God promises David a "house", a dynasty — a succession of kings descended from him. But also notice how the Lord says that one of David's descendants will build a house for God. Solomon literally built the temple — but Jesus builds an even better house or dynasty for His Father: the Church.

Check out 1 Peter 2 v 4–6

Wow. Pray!

81 – BLESSED IS BEST

Read Psalm 84 v 10–12

▣ *What big claim does the writer make? (v10)*

▣ *What does God do for His people? (v11)*

▣ *Who are God's people? (v12)*

God's people today (Christians) look to Jesus, not to a temple. He lives among us. We know He's put us on the way to eternal life — and a place for ever in His presence. And we know God doesn't hold anything good back from us, because He gave His Son, Jesus, to die in our place.

"Blessed" (or favoured) are those who...
• marvel at God's presence as they meet together.
• walk with Him on the road to eternal life.
• trust Him wholeheartedly.

82 – GOD'S GREAT KING

Check out a snapshot of the perfect King (and Bridegroom) in **Psalm 45 v 2–7**.

▷ *What's special about this royal bridegroom? (v2)*
▷ *Why is God impressed with him? (v7)*

This is one special king. Not only is he hugely impressive and wealthy (v8), he speaks graciously (v2) and fights for truth, justice and righteousness (v4, v6). God approves of him and lifts him above other kings. No prizes for guessing who this king reminds us of. But what about his bride?

▷ *How will the bride and her bridesmaids look on the wedding day? (v13–15)*
▷ *Why won't it be difficult for her to be loyal to the king? (v11)*
▷ *Who will praise the king and for how long? (v17)*

What a wedding. The rest of the Bible says these words about the groom (especially v6–7) are fulfilled in Jesus. Look again at v2–9 and 16–17. See how great He is?

What about the bride? Well, the New Testament tells us that the church (all believers) is Jesus' bride. One day the wedding will come and God's people will be fully united with Jesus, to live with the perfect King for ever. That's what I call a happy ending!

83 – BATTLE STATIONS

Read 1 Chronicles 20 v 1–3
It was at this time that David committed adultery and murder (see 2 Samuel 11 and 12). Chronicles isn't trying to hide David's failings (as chapters 13 and 21 show) — and Chronicles' readers would have known all about them. But it's highlighting David the *king* rather than David the *man*. Chronicles is all about God's kings, and looking forward to His perfect King.

84 – DON'T COUNT ON IT!

Read verses 1–2 again
Satan is mentioned by name just three times in the Old Testament (see also Zechariah 3 and Job 1–2). Now compare v1 with the same story in 2 Samuel 24 v 1. Contradictory? Nope, it's simply saying that behind this spiritual agent of evil, God reigns. Everything — including the devil — is ultimately in God's control.

Maybe David's sin here was a desire to see how great his empire had become... or taking pride in his skills as a general. Ironically, David's action in counting the military numbers led to a massive *reduction* in Israel's numbers (v14).

▷ *Are you prepared to admit your own vulnerability to temptation?*
▷ *Have you taken hold of the promise in James 4 v 7?*

Look at verses 17–19 again
▷ *What reason does David give the leaders for serving God? (v18)*
▷ *How enthusiastic should their response be? (v19a)*
▷ *Is it just emotional or should it be practical too? (v19b)*
▷ *Anything we can apply to ourselves here?*

Take a look at 1 Peter 2 v 9–12
▷ *How are Christians described in v9?*
▷ *What did we use to be?*
▷ *What are we now?*
▷ *What should our response to this wonderful grace be? (v11–12)*
▷ *Why? (v12)*

Check out **Acts 2 v 22–41** to see how Jesus exceeds David (and Solomon and all earthly kings).

▷ *When people ask us what Christianity means, what should be the content of our reply? (v22–24)*
▷ *What's God done for and through Jesus? (v32–33)*
▷ *What's God made Jesus? (v36)*

"Lord" means God Himself. "Christ" means God's eternal, all-powerful King. That's the firm fact about who Jesus is; so it's eternally important to respond in the right way.

Read 1 Thessalonians 5 v 23–24
Be encouraged.

What has the book of 1 Chronicles taught you? Take some time to look back over the book as a whole, perhaps underlining any parts that remind you of God's promises, His character or His way of dealing with sin. Then pray about what you've learned.

Read Romans 8 v 26–30
Believe it or not, Christians aren't happy all the time. We're still waiting for God's rescue plan to be completed. We're waiting to claim our inheritance in eternity with God. We cling on to this certain hope. As we groan our way through the suffering of this life, we struggle in prayer, barely knowing what to say to God sometimes. The Holy Spirit groans along with us. He understands, and helps us to pray.

Christians are people who love God — they've been called by Him as part of His perfect plans. And get this: God's at work. In all things. For the good of those who love Him. Our brief time of pain on this planet fits into God's eternal plans. We may not see it at the time, but God uses the hard things in life to do us good.

Read about David in a cave in
1 Samuel 24 v 1–22

engage wants to hear from YOU!

▶ Share experiences of God at work in your life.
▶ Any questions you have about the Bible or the Christian life?
▶ How can we make *engage* better?

Email us — **martin@thegoodbook.co.uk**

Or send us snail mail to: engage, Unit B1, Blenheim House,
1 Blenheim Road, Epsom, Surrey, KT19 9AP, UK

In the final engage

1 Peter No pain, no gain
2 Peter Think straight
2 Chronicles The good, the bad & the ugly
Proverbs Pursuing wisdom
Mark The end
Plus: Is hell real?
Friendship
Lots of other stuff we've not thought of yet

Order engage now!

Make sure you order the next issue of **engage**. Or even better, grab a one-year subscription to make sure **engage** lands in your hands as soon as it's out.

Call us to order in the UK on 0333 123 0880
International: +44 (0) 20 8942 0880

or visit your friendly neighbourhood website:
UK: www.thegoodbook.co.uk
N America: www.thegoodbook.com
Australia: www.thegoodbook.com.au
New Zealand: www.thegoodbook.co.nz

Growing
with God

Faithful, contemporary Bible reading resources for every age and stage.

NEW!

Beginning with God
For pre-schoolers

Table Talk & XTB
Table Talk for 4-11s and their parents, *XTB* for 7-11s

Discover
For 11-13s

Engage
For 14-18s

Explore
For adults

All Good Book Company Bible reading resources...

- have a strong focus on practical application
- encourage people to read the Bible for themselves
- explain Bible passages in context
- cover Bible books in the Old and New Testament

FREE *Explore* App for iOS and Android. Download today from the App Store or Android Market

UK: www.thegoodbook.co.uk
N America: www.thegoodbook.com
Australia: www.thegoodbook.com.au
New Zealand: www.thegoodbook.co.nz